US CONSUMER MARKET DEVELOPMENT

JOHN LOK

Copyright © John Lok
All Rights Reserved.

ISBN 979-888591482-6

This book has been published with all efforts taken to make the material error-free after the consent of the author. However, the author and the publisher do not assume and hereby disclaim any liability to any party for any loss, damage, or disruption caused by errors or omissions, whether such errors or omissions result from negligence, accident, or any other cause.

While every effort has been made to avoid any mistake or omission, this publication is being sold on the condition and understanding that neither the author nor the publishers or printers would be liable in any manner to any person by reason of any mistake or omission in this publication or for any action taken or omitted to be taken or advice rendered or accepted on the basis of this work. For any defect in printing or binding the publishers will be liable only to replace the defective copy by another copy of this work then available.

Contents

Foreword

Introduction

This book concerns how to apply behavioral economy and psychological methods to predict future America consumption market trend. I shall focus on only America future consumption market trend about five to ten years consumer behavioral psychological prediction as well as I shall give evidences to explain whether what factors cause the residents' consumption behavioral differences between big cities and small cities. In America consumption market, I shall indicate some popular American consumption market of some consumer products and foods as well as manufacturers' production of material consumption products to explain why and how the factors cause big and small cities' residents' consumption behavioral differences.

The first part explains how and why that what factors influence consumer behavioral differences between US big cities and small cities ,what factors can influence the Washington, New York big cities consumer behaviors, what is smart city digital technological living factor to influence Washington city residents' consumption behavioral changing , what factors influence US big cities and small cities same consumer behavioral habits

The second part indicates the manufacturers material and consumers product researching topics include: How to apply behavioral economy and psychological methods to predict future U.S. tobacco production, consumption and export trends? Is consumption in the United States influenced by income inequality? How to apply behavioral economy and psychological method to predict how to influence U.S. future consumption level by global climate warming target? What factors will influence U.S. long term trends in steel material consumption for manufacturing industries? What factors will influence how U.S. selected minerals changing trends in consumption and production for U.S. manufacturing industries? What factors will influence U.S. consumption of orange fruit and vegetables market? How can smart technologies influence U.S. consumers' purchase behaviors (consumption behaviors) of dairy categories of different product selections and consumption attitude changing? What factors will influence U.S. alcohol consumption in past, present and future trends? What factors will influence U.S. energy consumption user individual attitude changing on spending energy , such as petroleum and other liquids, natural gas, electricity generation on transportation , buildings and industrial useful aspects? What factors will influence U.S. wine and tea consumer drinking habit and purchasing behavior? What factors influence U.S. seafood and pork consumer eating behavior? What factors influence U.S. travelers change tourism entertainment behaviors? What factors influence U.S. food manufacturing material sugar supply and and demand? What factors influence U.S. daily lighting product market demand?

The final part applies demand and supply theory to explain what influences US nowadays consumer behavioral change.

The most important writing aim in my this books, I shall explain some evidences to support the cause and effect relationship is between U.S. people's consumption psychological attitude (cause) and consumption behavior (effect) to let my readers have more clear understanding how and why future these U.S. big and small cities consumption market will be influenced by these factors. All gathering data are based on U.S. past consumption market data to be used to predict how future U.S. these consumption markets change to achieve more accurate prediction.

Prologue

US big and small cities consumption differences

Factors influence consumer behavioral differences between US big cities and small cities

How and why do factors influence the consumer behavioral differences between US big and small cities? Has it consumer behavioral differences between US big and small cities? I shall indicate some evidences to attempt to explain whether it is possible that the consumer behavioral differences between US big and small cities as below:

For cosmetic product sale industry example, whether it has consumer behavioral differences between US big and small cities to influence US big and small cities residents whose consumption use for personal purpose. The major factors of cosmetic facial beauty product of price, attractive packing, sales promotion, advertisement, ingredients and warehouse storage factors will influence the US big cities and small cities resident consumers' attitudes and choice consumption behavioral differences. It is due to the sale method difference of sale price, ingredients, promotion method and warehouse storage number to cosmetic products when the cosmetic consumers choose to buy any brands of cosmetic products from small cities or big cities in US.

In fact, cosmetics are not just used by the US young female resident customer any longer, US young male resident customer is increasing taking as the use of more and more body sprays, perfumes and other cosmetics. Hence, the US resident young female and male both young cosmetic product buyer number will influence the cosmetic product sale number in

US big and small cities. For example, if the US big or small cities have many adult older age male or female residents are living more than the younger age male or female residents in US. Then, the US resident cosmetics consumer will reduce. Otherwise, if US big or small cities have many US younger age male or female residents are living more than the older age. Then, the US itself US resident cosmetics consumer number will raise in possible. The reason is because cosmetics product need is depended on age factor. So, younger age US big or small cities residents will have more facial beauty need to more than older age US residents who is living in either US big cities or small cities. Such as US cosmetic product sale case, the large or small cities cosmetic product sale number will be extremely depended on whether how any younger or older age US residents who are living in the either big or small cities in US.

Based on this age factor reason, the age factor is more important to influence US big or small cities cosmetic product sale number more than other factors, such as price, brand, promotion ingredients etc. different cosmetic products themselves basic product sale method factors. Also, it implies that the US large or small cities cosmetic facial beauty product sale number will not be possible to be influenced the sale number to be reduces, even the brand of cosmetics product sale price is raised, if the US large or small cities have many younger age US residents are living more than older age US residents number who are living in US. Hence, in consumer behavioral view point, it seems to explain that the age factor is extremely important to influence the US big cities or small cities cosmetics product sale number.

Another one for luxury fashion sale industry example, whether it has consumer behavioral differences between big cities and small cities in US. In fact, luxury fashion industry, it has low or high luxury quality difference. This quality factor will influence US resident consumption behaviors between big cities and small cities in US.

The luxury sector can be categorized under three categories: The common luxury fashion product, which include gold, watches, mobile phones, hand bags, computers and wine and more. The second category is the more expensive high or low quality of luxury cars, and the third category is the luxury services, which include the living hotel services , tourism etc. entertainment services.

In US, the large and small cities resident age, gender, and occupation and income levels are different, so these factors can influence the buying intention of luxury watches and mobile phones, gold, wine etc. luxury products and luxury entertainment needs and different kinds of luxury products and / or luxury entertainment consumption behaviors with respect to US different regions.

In fact, although the US big cities have larger population amount to compare the small cities. But, it is not the main reason to influence the US large or small cities any kinds of luxury product sale number or entertainment service number any one. If the US large cities, e.g. Washington, New York both have many high income , better or permanent occupation , high education young people are living in these cities. Although, these both cities have larger population amount to compare the small cities. The population number factor ought not influence the both US large cities' luxury fashion product or luxury entertainment service consumers number to be increased if these both big cities have many low educational level, many temporary or contact job employees who are living in these both big cities in US. Otherwise, it is possible that the other small cities' cosmetic product consumer number will be more than these both big cities in US, if other small cities have many residents who have high stable income, permanent jobs and high educational level occupation and high educational level young residents are living in small cities in US. So, it seems that the larger population number factor is not the main influential factor to cause the different kinds of luxury fashion product or luxury entertainment service sale number to raise the luxury consumption need in US large cities. It depends on whether how many high education, high income and stable permanent occupation residents who are living in either big cities or small cities in US every year. So, the influential factor to US big cities or small cities luxury fashion every kind of product or luxury entertainment service sale number ought be the how many US resident individual has high education level , high income, better and stable or permanent occupation factor which can influence the luxury fashion product or luxury entertainment service changing every year in US.

On online shopping customer behavior example, whether what factors which can influence the more or less frequent online shopping consumption behavioral difference between big cities and small cities in US. Although, online shopping behaviors are popular in US and internet technology can influence many US resident consumers choose to apply internet to buy any product habitually. IS saving time or convenience the main factor which influence US resident consumers choose to internet to buy any things ? If it is not right, whether what other factors influence US big or small cities resident consumers choose internet to buy any things from online purchase channel habitually?

In fact, the most popular online shopping products which are books, watches, electronic product, sport products, home using product, e.g. tooth paste, towel, movie or music or entertainment game videos, electronic air tickets products. So, it implies that other kinds of products are not popular to be chosen to buy from internet. So, it explains that it does not mean that the US big cities have more population number to compare small cities. It does not mean that big cities must have many online shoppers number to compare small cities in US. For example, in the year, if the US big or small cities have many resident customers who have needs to choose to buy any kinds of above products. Then, the online shoppers number will possible increase in the year. Otherwise, in the year, if the US big or small cities have many resident customers who have not any more needs to choose to buy any kinds of above products. Then, the online shoppers number will possible decrease in the year.

Is saving time and convenience the most influential factor to cause big cities and small cities US resident consumers to choose online shopping? In US cig cities, it is possible that time saving can influence big cities residents to choose to buy any kinds of products from internet. If the large city resident who are living so far away from the sellers' shops. He/she will consider whether he/she needs to spend how long time to go to the shop to buy the product , when he/she is busy at the moment. He/she will need to choose either catching any transportation tools or driving himself/ herself car to spend long time to arrive the shop to buy the kind of product or turning on computer to click the shop's website to buy the product from internet online sale channel at home. Thus, the US big city resident consumer will be persuaded to choose online channel to buy the product attractively when he/she has computer and internet supplying at home as well as the seller has website to provide any US resident consumers to click whose website to buy any things. So, it is possible that saving time and convenience factor can influence the US big cities busy resident customers to choose buy the products from internet at homes. Otherwise, in US small cities , it is not time saving factor can influence small cities US residents to choose to buy any kinds of products from internet easily. If the small city US resident is living near to the shop, he/she can walk to the shop in short time. Then, he /she will still choose to walk the shop to visit because he/she touch the product, sees the product actually, compares the product and other kinds or similar products prices and images. Otherwise, internet can only satisfy the online shopper's picture showing feeling, it is difficult to compare other similar products prices and shapes actually as well as the online shopper can not walk to the shop to feel the actual shopping environment whether the product is actual need or is not actual need to satisfy whose need. So, the online shopping channel ought not influence the US small cities resident consumers to choose to buy the product easily when the/she is not busy and his/her home is near to the shop, so he/she does not need to catch any kinds of transportation tools or drive car to go to the shop. So, saving time and convenience factor is the influential factor to cause the US small cities resident consumers to choose to buy the product from internet, unless the seller has not shop to let the consumer to visit to buy the product. Hence, it implies that the distance between the US small city resident's house and the seller's shop which will be one influential factor to persuade the US small city resident to decide whether online shopping is suitable to him/her more or visiting shop is suitable to him/her more.

Consequently, online shopping consumption behaviors must not extremely be chosen to all different regional US small and big cities residents. It depends on saving time, convenience and the distance between the resident's house and the seller's shop and whether the resident is busy when he/she feels need to buy any things in US.

CHAPTER TWO

Factors can influence the Washington, New York big cities consumer behaviors

In US, there are many cities residents, they have different cultural level , different population, different living habits, different entertainment activities needs , different living styles , different educational level who are living in US big or small cities nowadays. SO, I believe that any one of these factors which will influence their consumption desires to choose or decide to buy which kinds of foods to eat, which products to use, even which kinds of entertainment choices to satisfy their need in their daily necessary needs to cause their consumption behaviors have more different between US bog and small cities. I shall focus on Washington, New York both US big cities to explain how these factors to influence these both cities residents' consumption behaviors are different to other small cities in US.

US, Census Bureau population estimates,(2011-2013) indicates that US Washington and New York cities, these both cities have total population 195, 302 . The population by race and ethnicity includes 71% Hispanic, 17% white, 7 % black, 3 % Asian, and 1% others. So, these both cities have different race and cultural and living habits of people are living in these both big cities in US. They have about 48% people are foreign born and they have also 39% have limited English proficiency.

On housing quality demand aspect, although US Washington and New York are large cities, but due to many low educational level and low income people who are living in Washington and New York cities. So, these people whose housing living demand are nor high, poorly maintained housing is associated with negative health outcomes, these low education level and low income level neighborhood relationship and conditions will be worse than the high educational level and income level people who are living in Washington and New York cities as well as these low educational level and income level householder home consumers are living in poor hosing environment, it will bring illnesses, include asthma and respiratory illnesses, injuries and poor mental health. SO, this poor living environment factor will influence this low educational and low income level householders who reduce consumption desires and do less consumption behaviors frequently, although they are living in Washington, New York big cities developed country nowadays. Moreover, Washington and New York cities' air pollution level is higher to compare other cities. It is possible due to factories manufacturing, cars emission to cause air pollution in these both cities as well as it will bring Washington and New York cities' residents to consider health problems, particularly among the young, seniors and those with pre-existing health conditions.

So, air pollution factor will influence Washington and New York cities' householders who begin to consider health issues. Every family will be possible to be influenced to not buy more than car at home, even none any cars are purchased to be keep at home. They will choose to catch public transportation tools, e.g. buses, trams, underground trains, taxis, ferries to go to offices or any working places or travelling places for entertainment or working aims. Thus, air pollution will bring that none cars behavioral consumption or activities will be more popular choice to Washington and New York cities residents. Because they won't hope to live in one dirty air pollution city in US. But rental cars activities will be possible increased, due to the US Washington and New York cities owning car householders who should possible sell their cars as well as the they will choose rent cars to go to anywhere for working or entertainment needs every day habitually. Then, the renting car businesses will be possible influenced to increase, due to air pollution factor influences to change Washington and New York residents' driving activities to be reduced.

On tobacco retail environment aspect, NYC DOHMH bureau of vital statistics, (2003-2012) indicates that the prevalence of tobacco retailers in Washington, New York tobacco retailers are similar to the prevalence citywide, supermarket access to also similar to access citywide, with 119 square feet per 100 people. Why does tobacco retailers number can be still more? It is possible that there are many low education and low income different race people who do not concern health issue. SO, they can not change their smoking habits to continue to buy tobacco to smoke.

Otherwise, the high education and high income people who begin to concern health issue. So, they will avoid to buy more tobacco to smoke or they will choose to buy the electronic tobacco to replace tobacco to smoke, even they will attempt to avoid to buy any tobacco to smoke habitually.

Hence, the tobacco consumption level will not be reduced to the low education and low income tobacco smoking consumers group, but the tobacco consumption level will be influenced to be reduced to the high income and high educational level tobacco smoking consumers group because they begin to concern health issue from air pollution serious feeling consequence and brings the reason explains that why it will have many high educational and income people choose to avoid to consume any tobacco in Washington and New York big cities. So, air pollution factor will be one influential factor to change the high educational level and income peoples' tobacco smoking behaviors to either smoke electronic tobacco to replace tobacco or avoid to buy any tobacco or electronic tobacco to smoke when they are living in Washington or New York city US.

On Washington and New York adult education factor how to influence the cities' consumer behavioral aspect, US, Census Bureau population estimates, (2013) indicates that over a third of adults in Washington and New York cities have college degrees, but a high percentage have not completed high school about 39%. Why does education factor will influence Washington and New York cities US consumer behaviors. The reason is simple because if the both cities have many high educational level are living, then they will have possible to earn high income and it can influence their consumption efforts to be raised.

Such as the Washington and New York income factor, although it has over a third of adults in Washington and New York have college degrees , so it seems this a third of adults who have effort often to consume as well as they will buy more expensive and high quality products to use or choose any high price and proving high food quality of restaurants or consume any high price of entertainment activities, often going to cinemas to watch movies, playing golf sports , buying expensive bicycles , buying expensive watches or computer etc. luxury products, buying expensive cars to drive , often travelling etc. different luxury entertainment activities in order to satisfy their enjoyable aims. SO, they have important role to bring consumption effort to be raised in Washington and New York cities. Otherwise, there are many people who have not completed the high schools. Hence, their income will be lesser. Then they won't like to go to shopping option, instead of eating , living basic essential every day living necessary. So, these low education level people will be influenced to reduce entertainment consumption when they are still living in Washing or New York cities.

Hence, in Washington and New York cities, the living in poverty limits healthy lifestyle choices and makes it difficult to access health care and resources that can promote health and prevent illness to this low income people in Washington or New York city US. The low income people will often only consider their health issue more than entertainment issue, e.g. they need to pay more medical expenditure to avoid illnesses or death, then they will consider that whether they ought need to buy medical insurance to reduce their future medical expenditure burden and they will save more money to bank to prepare their medical insurance expenditure in long term. Hence, the low income and low educational factor will also influence the low income people's life quality or lifestyle to be go down, instead of reducing consumption desires influencer to them.

However, Washington and New York cities' rent are also more than other cities in US as well as unemployment and unaffordable housing are also closely associated with poverty and poor health to Washington and New York cities' low income people consumer group. However, Washington and New York cities will need have many young residents who to live. This expensive rent factor will also influence their consumption desire in Washington and New York cities US. So, in economic stress view point, the poverty , low education, low income, unemployment and rent burden factors will influence Washington and New York cities' low education young residents' consumption desires to be reduced nowadays.

On Washington and New York cities birth rate influence aspect, it will also influence further long term Washington and New York residents' consumer number. IN Washington and New York cities, the rate of preterm births is a key driver to influence future Washing ton and New York cities' customer number. The reason is simple, if current Washington and New York cities have many young parents who choose to born many babies. Then , it will have many adults in these both cities in the future. When the parents will need to buy many toys to let their children to play and foods for their children to eat. SO, the toys and children foods need number will be influenced to increase suddenly when these both cities sudden increase born number. When they are growing, they will need entertainment, e.g. riding bicycles sport, playing basket ball, football sports, going to cinemas to watch movies, going to music halls to listen music or song. So, any entertainment products e.g. cars, or performance needs will increase when these babies are growing to young age stage. Even, they must need to go to school to study. So, the studying needs will increase and they will bring many schools need in Washington and New York cities. Hence, the birth rate will influence the future entertainment needs and education needs demand to Washington and New York big cities' residents consumption market.

On car rental service aspect, in Washington and New ,York cities, the car rental service is very convenient, there are many car rental service supplies are located to close anywhere householders' houses. So, when the householder feels that he/she has travelling or driving entertainment activity need. He /she can walk to the rent car service provider to compare whose rent car service fee in order to choose which car service provider fee is the most reasonable , or cheaper and car quality is safe. Then, he/she will choose to rent the car to go to anywhere to enjoy in holidays. So, when the Washington , New Yorker feels that he/she has travelling or driving entertainment need, when will choose to rent car to drive conveniently. The convenient car rent service factor will influence many Washington , New Yorkers to choose rent car to drive frequently and habitually. Moreover, many Washington and New Yorkers feel their cities' air pollution is serious, they will choose to rent cars to replace to drive themselves cars to avoid air pollution challenge will be caused to raise. So, car rental service needs will be influenced to raised, due to many residents feel air pollution is serious in Washington and New York cities. So, air pollution brings the car rent service and transportation tools service need to be raised, but the car purchase need will be decreased in Washington and New York cities US.

On public transportation tools influence aspect, in Washington and New York cities , although subway and bus trips significantly outnumber for hire vehicle trips, for hire vehicles provide some services that the mass transit system can't. Many Washington and New York cities residents use for hire vehicles when subway or bus lines are too far away from their homes or destination or when mass transit is perceived as too slow or requires too long a wait.

IN addition to convenience and speed, passengers may also select for hire vehicles for comfort , privacy and the relative ease of transporting bulk items and packages. Moreover, most Washington and New York residents get around using subways or buses. Public transit makes up the largest part of Washington , New York city transportation system by ridership, but taxi service has significant role. SO, although air pollution will influence bus , ferry , underground train, tram public transportation tools needs much. Due to they choose to sell their private vehicles or they choose to walk to avoid often driving cars to influence Washington, New York cities air to be more polluted, but the taxi need is not needed vey much, they won't prefer to choose taxi transportation tool to catch. It is possible due to taxi fee is charged higher than other general public transportation tools in Washington, New York cities US. So, Washington and New York cities air pollution won't influence taxi service need to increased significantly.

In the future, Washington and New York residents will continue to consider air pollution challenge. So, the Washington and New York cities public transportation service will trend to have the lowest rate of private car ownership in the nation, instead of New York , Washington cities and the highest utilization of for –hire services. Every day Washington, New York residents and tourists take trips in-for-hire vehicles, relying on them to get to work, school, medical appointments to and from the airports and other destinations. Hence, future New York and Washington cities residents will depend on public transport tools or vehicle rent services more than to drive themselves owning vehicles to go to anywhere often, when they begin to consider air pollution challenge in their both large cities US.

It seems that these both big cities, US public transportation tools and vehicle rent service needs will be increased . Even , future these both big cities' transportation tools and vehicle rent service price will be raised, their higher price won't influence these both cities residents to choose to catch them to go to anywhere because they will consider future air pollution serious challenge will be increased from their frequent driving behavioral cause.

In the minimum wage eliminating aspect, how the minimum wage eliminating factor influence Washing and New York cities residents consumption desires. How and why can minimum wage implementation factor influence Washington , New York residents consumption desires to be raise or decreased.

Nowadays, US minimum wage is $15 per hour. If either the minimum wage $15 per hour increases that it will influence whether the Washington or New York residents will increase consumption desire or the minimum wage $15 per hour decreases whether the Washington , New York residents will decrease consumption desire. It is one interesting consumer psychological question to concern whether Washington, New York residents will be influenced to reduce or raise consumption desires when minimum wage $15 per hour is either raised or decreased in US.

In fact, the low income US Washington, New York residents need have the minimum wage to protect their every day living benefit or welfare to have more confidence to consume much. Although, Washington, New York cities are US main capital cities, but their life level , eg. Housing price is generally higher than the other small cities in US. SO, if the low income Washington, New York workers are eliminated the minimum income protection or reduced the per hour wage is below than $15 per hour. I believe that it will influence their consumption desires to be fallen down. SO, their daily essential necessary expenditures will be influenced to raise. Otherwise, if minimum wage $15 per hour can be raised to more than this level. Then, it will encourage Washington, New York residents low income residents' consumption desires to be raised. So, I feel the minimum wage raising or falling factor will influence Washington , York low income residents' consumption desires to be increased or decreased influentially , due to these cities have high housing rent and entertainment expenditure and food expenditure to compare other cities in US.

CHAPTER THREE

Smart city digital technological living factor influence Washington city residents' consumption behavioral changing

Can smart city digital technological living factor influence Washington city residents' consumption behavioral changing? Smart technologies in order help Washington city's consumption residents to go to shopping more easily or conveniently. Smart Washington city add digital intelligence to existing when systems, making it possible to help Washington residents to apply mobile technology to find the accurate shopping locations more easily. Even, they can bring mobile to buy anything, what their mobiles link to themselves visa cards. Then, they go to the retailers to put on their mobile phones on retailers' counters. Then, their mobile phones can help them to pay to buy the products, due to their visa card had connected to their mobiles. So, Washington city residents do not need bring cash or visa cards. They can choose to bring mobiles to go to shopping after their mobiles had connected to their banks' visa card number for payment records. It is very convenient and safe to Washington residents to buy mobiles to go to anywhere to shopping. So, they won't often worry cash losses or visa cards losses, when they leave their homes. It is possible to encourage Washington residents to raise consumption desires.

If Washington city can have these high technological products to be installed to their householders. It is possible to encourage them to go out shopping often. When they feel their houses' security is very safe. So, when the householders install their high technological security tools in their houses, e.g. real-time mapping gunshot detection, smart surveillance, emergency response optimization, body-warn cameras, disaster early-warning systems, personal alert applications, home security systems, data-driven building inspections etc. different security equipment at houses. Then, it will encourage Washington city residents often to leave their houses because they will feel thieves are difficult to enter their houses to steel thing in their houses. Also, if Washington residents can install high technological energy saving equipment at their homes. Then, it will encourage them to use more electrical appliances for entertainment needs, cooking needs etc. activities at homes, due to they will feel energy expenditure will reduce when they install any kinds of energy saving equipment at homes.

They include building automation systems, have energy automation systems, home energy consumption tracking, dynamic electricity pricing tracking system and every distribution automation systems. Their new energy saving equipment will encourage Washington residents to spend more time to use any energy consumption equipment or cooking or watching television or listening music or turning on lights any necessary activities, when they stay at themselves homes any times. So, if Washington can be changed to improve to be one smart high technological entertainment, life intention city. Then, it will encourage Washington residents' homing enjoyment desired need to br increased as well as consumption desired need to be increased both. So, smart city high technological factor can be one important factor to persuade or encourage or influence Washington residents to choose to spend more time to go out to shopping or carry on entertainment activity at homes often in possible.

In US, big cities, such as Washington, New York , their population must more than small cities. Although, US have high population who are living in big cities. However, it is not represent that high big cities population must have many customer number more than small cities. Otherwise, US small cities will have possible more customer number to compare large cities for some kinds of products or services. What factors can influence US, big cities and small cities residents' consumption behaviors are different. I shall explain the factors as below:

The politics of mass consumption in US big cities and small cities residents' consumption habitual factor. Historians and social scientists has researched on the political and social impact of mass consumption on nowadays century America. They indicate the culture, social and political different factors between US large cities and small cities, which will influence the mass consumer behaviors and markets difference. For example, in cultural difference view point, US big cities residents can be more acceptable to buy any new kinds of products more than US small cities residents. So, for any kinds of new products the US big cities residents will be the major customers more than the US small cities residents , due to their cultural level , educational level are influenced more acceptable to use any new products changing attitudes more easily than small cities residents in US.

Otherwise, US small cities residents who have much traditional minds and attitudes and they can not accept to use any new kinds of products. So, US big cities and small cities residents' cultural and educational level and living habits are different. This factor can influence US big cities and small cities residents whose consumption behaviors to any new kinds of products. Hence, it seems that US big cities' any kinds of new products can be sold more easily than US small cities' any kinds of new products. It means brand, price, quality factors to new kinds of products are not the most influential factors to US big and small cities consumers to choose to buy. The US big and small cities' cultural level difference will seem be the main influential factor to influence US residents to choose to buy any kinds of new products nowadays. So, if the new product provider can change US small cities residents' traditional attitudes to accept to use any kinds of new products. Then, the US small cities' new product supplier can raise its sale effort more easily in possible.

The other factor is that segmentation of U big cities and small cities teenagers in terms of their buying behaviors and attitudes towards commercial consumption are different. For example, the US big cities and small cities teenagers' commercial valuables are different. It means that the US big cities teenagers have higher commercial valuables to every products. Their demands to each product's using value, quality value will be higher to compare the US small cities teenagers. So, they prefer to choose to buy more expensive products because they feel that they have higher commercial valuables to compare cheaper products. Otherwise, the US small cities teenagers who have lower commercial valuables to any products. So, they prefer to choose to buy cheaper products, because they will feel cheaper products have lower commercial valuables in generally.

So, it implies that higher commercial valuable products ought be chosen to sell to big cities market in US , e.g. mobile phones, cars, yachts, computers, heaters, air conditioners etc. high commercial valuable housing using or entertainment products. Otherwise, lower commercial valuable products ought be chosen to sell to small cities market in US, e.g. books, movie or music , song cd, DVD , stationery , bicycle, school bags etc. entertainment products or learning using products for students teenager group consumers. Moreover, the teenagers will be these using or entertainment products main customers. This teenager customer target customer group will have more needs to buy entertainment products to enjoy, e.g. purchase cd or dvd listening music, watching movie entertainment products or going to cinemas to watch movies or music halls to listen music entertainment services as well as they need to buy books and stationery for going to schools to learn necessary. So, the teenagers customer number for low commercial valuable product in small cities , US will be higher to compare the teenagers customer number in large cities, US in possible or the teenagers or student target market share is higher than older age people in US small cities. However, the low commercial valuable learning using products, e.g. books, stationery this kind of reading products will be any teenagers' (students) whose reading needs. So, books will be their essential reading products or necessary needs. Also, teenagers are popular to consider their beauty or smart clothing. So, the low commercial valuable products, e.g. clothes, face beauty products will be popular consumption products in US, small cities.

Consequently, the consumption difference between large cities and small cities , US. The low commercial valuable products ought be more popular to need to buy to the teenagers in small cities , US. Otherwise, the high commercial valuable product ought be more popular to need to buy to the adult consumers in big cities.

3.1 Factors influence US big cities and small
cities same online consumer behavioral habits

US , online (electronic commerce) environmental factor can influence US inner city shopping areas face a decreasing number of visitors and declining sales numbers to the visiting shops of consumers' buying habits, but US online purchase habits to online shoppers sales numbers and the number of online shoppers will increase. Because e-commerce and young aging online consumers are considered to be the main causes in US inner city shopping areas, due the US traditional visiting shop consumers' habits are influenced to choose to buy any products from online by internet technology, however in US big cities or small cities. What Factors can influence US big cities and small cities' consumers change their traditional visiting shopping areas habits to online visiting consumption habits.

Improving the buying experience in inner-city shopping areas may be a solution to attract more visitors to choose traditional visiting shopping areas habits more easily in US big cities and small cities. How to change US big cities and small cities young aging online consumption behaviors to traditional visiting shopping areas habits? I believe US big cite or small cities businesses need to change their shops or stores historical appearances, shopping locations, appeared appearances, shop windows and advertisement designs in order to attract US young aging shoppers to choose to visit to their ship or stores habitually. Because , online shopping method had attracted US big cities or small cities young aging to use internet channel to buy anything at homes conveniently. Due to US some big and small cities of businesses stores (shops) which are located so far from some big cities or small cities' young age residents' houses. So, it causes their needs to catch buses or taxi or trams or trains , underground trains etc. transportation tools, or driving their cars to visit any shopping areas to buy anythings. So, internet can influence US big cities or small cities young age residents to buy anything from internet at homes conveniently.

Hence, if US big cities or small cities some businesses hope their shops or stores can attract many young aging US residents to choose to visit their stores or shops to buy any things. They need to change their shop design to be more attractive, e.g. providing more comfortable furniture to visitors to sit, changing the shop internal areas' hot temperature and white light shop environment to the warm temperature and colorful light shop environment to raise their shop inner environment more attractive, changing their shopping location , e.g. moving their shops from narrow street (less pedestrians) to busy precinct (more pedestrians) or moving their shops to near to transportation tool stations, e.g. underground train stations, bus stations, taxi stations, train stations, tram stations etc. stations in large or small cities' main streets, e.g. office, restaurant, large size shopping centers locations. Hence, it seems that shop location and shop inner shopping environment factor will influence the US big cities or small cities residents to change their consumption behaviors whether they ought choose to visit shopping areas more or visit website to consume at home more.

Reference

Overall population, race and age: US, Census Bureau population estimates, 2013: Foreign born and English proficiency: US Census Bureau, American community survey, 2011-2013.

Self reported health: WYC DOHMH community health survey, 2011-2013, life expectancy: NYC DOHMH bureau of vital statistics, 2003-2012

US global consumption behaviors

What factors will affect future U.S. people consumer behavior of purchasing to tobacco products

Nowadays, U.S. cigarette manufacturers have been increasing the use of less expensive foreign tobacco and decreasing the use of more costly U.S. grown tobacco. Hence, it is possible to cost U.S.. cigarette quality is worse, due to cigarette is manufactured more cheap and high quality of tobacco to cause the U.S. cigarette price can be cheaper and high quality to compare other countries' cigarette to attract global cigarette consumers to buy more easier. However, the high educational level and high income population in big cities is more than the small cities in US. This high income and high educational US residents will concern their health, so they will concern to smoke cigarette whether how their smoking behaviors will bring harm to their bodies. So, the cigarette smoking number in big cities, US seems to be less than the small cities, US.

IS it only cheaper cigarette price factor to attract many cigarette consumers to choose to buy any U.S. brands of cigarette manufacturers' cigarette to smoke? Has it other factors to lead global cigarette consumers to choose to buy any brands of U.S. cigarette to smoke? It is one interesting researching question. I shall indicate that the other different factors which can influence global cigarette consumers why they prefer to choose to buy any U.S. brands of cigarettes to smoke, instead of cheap price and high quality smoking reason as below:

On U.S. government assistance to encourage tobacco industry development hand, U.S. government helps farmers to shift to alternative agricultural enterprises, non-farm business development, training for non-farm occupations, household income support, and possibly even support for the social service that will suffer with a shifting tobacco economy.

So, on behavioral economic view point, U.S. government creates many non-farm occupations to work in tobacco and cigarette non-farming industry. So, it influences many tobacco and cigarette manufacturers have confidence to develop their cigarette manufacturing and sale business in U.S. Due to many cigarette manufacturers sudden manufacture many cigarette number to supply in U.S. domestic market, even overseas market. But, U.S. domestic people number is small, so U.S. cigarette consumer demand number must be less than overseas cigarette export number.

In supply and demand theory, when the product supply number is more than the consumer demand number, then it will cause the product's price to be fallen down. So, such as cigarette case, when U.S. government subsidizes fund to assist U.S. cigarette manufacturer to develop their cigarette business to encourage them to research different kinds taste of cigarette to grow in non-farming industry. It will lead many cigarette manufacturers compete in U.S. domestic market. Moreover, due to different kinds of U.S. cigarette supply number is more than U.S. domestic cigarette buyer number. Hence, it will cause U.S. domestic cigarette sellers to reduce cigarette sale price in order to attract many cigarette consumers to choose to buy themselves brand of cigarette to smoke. Hence, U.S.'s domestic cigarette supply number is more than cigarette consumer demand number.

This factor will also lead U.S. domestic cigarette manufacturers to choose to reduce themselves cigarette price in order to attract many cigarette consumers to choose to buy themselves brand of cigarette to smoke. Hence, U.S. cigarette consumer individual behavior will influence cigarette industry economic growth. It is depending on whether how many U.S. cigarette consumers accept to smoke cigarette if many U.S. cigarette consumers feel it is not health product to influence their health to be worse when they had been smoking long term. Then, the U.S. cigarette economic development will be poor. So, U.S. domestic cigarette consumer' health attitudes will influence their cigarette purchase behaviors. It implies that if many U.S. cigarette consumers consider their health, then the U.S. cigarette consumers number will be decreased to influence U.S. cigarette industry income will be also decreased.

Although, U.S. government can spend money to subsidize cigarette manufacturers to develop their cigarette manufacturing industry. But it is not represent the cigarette manufacturers can succeed to raise to sell their cigarette number. Because U.S. domestic cigarette consumer individual health attitude will influence U.S. cigarette sale number, even they are good taste and famous brand and cheap price factor.

Every U.S. cigarette manufacturers choose to sell extra many cigarettes to overseas market. But, it is not guaranty to sell more easily. Because if overseas cigarette consumers feel cigarette product can bring harm to influence their health when they smoke long time. Then, their negative attitude to smoke cigarette which will influence they choose not to buy any brands of U.S. cigarettes to smoke. Even, cheap price, famous brand, good taste factor, they can not attract them to buy. So, cigarette consumers' negative or positive smoking cigarette feeling or attitude factor which will influence cigarette consumers to choose to buy any brands of U.S. cigarette to smoke. Consequently, I conclude that how to change global cigarette consumers to positive smoking attitude or feeling from negative cigarette smoking feeling or attitude, that is one important factor to lead U.S. cigarette industry in success.

I shall indicate what factors can affect global consumer behavior of purchasing U.S. tobacco products as below:

On the one hand, I believe that the major determinants of U.S. tobacco product demand, in particular the relationship between tobacco demand and the price of tobacco products and global consumer income level. For example, if global many tobacco consumers feel to smoke any U.S. brand of tobacco products, they influence their bodies to be not health. Then, their negative attitude to smoke any U.S. tobacco products which will influence they do not buy any U.S. brands of tobacco products to smoke more again.

It will lead global tobacco product consumers' demand to buy any kinds of U.S. tobacco products to be decreased and it has relationship to lead any U.S. brands of price of tobacco products need to be fallen down in order to attract the consideration of tobacco products poor health influence of consumers have desire to buy any U.S. brands of tobacco products to smoke. Because any U.S. brands of tobacco products had brought damage health image to global tobacco consumers to choose to buy this country's any brands of tobacco products.

On the other hand, if the global tobacco habiting smoking consumers' income of level is falling down, due to global economic environment goes down and many businesses liquidate factor. It will cause many people unemployed. Then, the global level of income going down factor, it will also influence the tobacco habiting smoking consumers' smoking needs to be decreased. It means that the different U.S. brands of tobacco sale number will be possible reduced, because global tobacco habiting smoking consumers' income of level is falling down as the same time.

Thus, determinants of consumer demand for any U.S. brands of tobacco products which include these factors as below:

Price of the tobacco product; disposable income of the consumer; demographic characteristics of the country's population (e.g. gender, age, ethic). For example, of the country has every old age people more than young age people, then the tobacco product consumer number will be less than another country has young age people number more than old age people number; socio -economic status of the country's population (e.g. education, occupation, employment status). For example, of the country has many high educatin and professional occupation people, then the U.S. brands of tobacco product consumer number will be decreased, due to they are possible considerate their health , due to their health psychology will influence them to accept to smoke any tobacco products any more; rural versus urban area of residence in the country, if the country has many people are living in urban area of residence more than rural are of residence. Then, it will lead many tobacco product consumers, due to urban area has more shopping malls which can encourage tabacco products to buy in anywhere convenient places in the countries' cities. Otherwise, rural area will not have more shopping malls to provide tobacco products to let the rural residents to buy easily; tobacco control intervention (e.g. smoking restrictions, bans on advertising influence tobacco consumer number). If the country government had achieved new smoking prohibition legislation to prohibit young age people to buy, then the country will reduce the young age tobacco product consumers number; knowledge and information about the health efforts of tobacco use will be one negative smoking any tobacco products of education media to bring negative not health tobacco smoking attitude or psychology to influence the country's people to buy any tobacco products to smoke. Hence, all above of these any one psychological and economic factors will influence global consumers to buy any U.S. brands of tobacco products to smoke.

Based on above all factors, I believe that seems U.S. future tobacco export market development trend is that U.S. any brands of tobacco (cigarette product) price will need to be fallen down, due to global tobacco consumers' consideration to long term tobacco smoking behavior will influence poor health as well as future global income level will be possible fallen down factors, due to global economic environment will be poor suddenly and un-predictive. So, their un-predictive poor economic environment factor will cause many businesses liquate to cause many people unemployed in different countries.

In conclude that future these both un-predictive factors: Such as un-predictive when global poor economic environment factor and un-predictive factor when global many people consideration to smoke cigarette (tobacco) products negative psychological emotion raising factor. These both factors will influence U.S. cigarette (tobacco) price to be influenced to fall down because these both factors will influence global cigarette (tobacco) smoker number to be reduced. Hence, future U.S. any brands of cigarette (tobacco) product manufacturers or sellers, if they still expected to keep cigarette (tobacco) sale price to be raised or remain to the same sale price level. Then, they need to make accurate prediction when these both bad factors influence to global cigarette (tobacco) consumer demand to smoke cigarette number to be reduced to reach the serious minimum number level in order to plan any solutions to avoid cigarette (tobacco) consumer number to be reduced to the serious minimum number level, due to these both negative economic environment and negative smoking tobacco or cigarette factors will influence the global smoking cigarette or tobacco product of consumer number to be decreased. Thus, I suggest that the brand of U.S. tobacco or cigarette manufacturers need to considerate how to manufacture the health ingredient of tobacco or cigarette products to let global tobacco or cigarette consumers believe that their health won't be poor when they smoke the brand of U.S. tobacco or cigarette products. So, it implies that health factor will be the most important to influence global tobacco or cigarette consumers to choose to buy any U.S. brands of tobacco or cigarette products to smoke in the future.

CHAPTER FIVE

How can global climate changing and global population income level raising factor influence future U.S. greenhouse gas consumption behavior

I suppose US big cities have more high income and high education people are living. So, they have more effort to buy greenhouse gas to use at home to reduce pollution challenge. So, it seems that the greenhouse gas sale number in big cities, US will be higher than the small cities, US. Whether will future global climate change influence U.S. consumption market to reduce U.S. people greenhouse gas consumption desire? Does external natural environment variable factor influence U.S. people's green house gas consumption desires to be reduced? Ought U.S. businessmen need to achieve international poor or negative climate warm environment changing policies to prevent future U.S. natural energy resource shortage challenge causing? The important question concerns why and when future global climate warm environment changing negative factor will influence global natural energy , such as greenhouse gas consumption desire to be fallen down. I shall explain why and how global warm climate change will influence global consumption desires to be reduced as below:

On the one hand, I shall explain how and why global warming climate changing factor will influence future greenhouse gas consumers' useful desires to be reduced. For national and regional greenhouse gas daily nature energy global home users' consumption product example, the emission reduction, due to global climate warm changing factor causes, it will lead global home users' consumption desires to be reduced. In general, global home energy consumers will choose to buy greenhouse gas energy product for these functions: Cooking food, driving vehicles to travel, air condition and heater energy supply etc. main daily basic needs at home or driving uses. So, when the home energy users (families) need to drive cars to go to office or go to any where to entertain needs. These families will choose to buy greenhouse gas to drive cars to replace other kinds of energy. Also, when families choose to cook breakfast, lunch or dinner at home, who will make choice either buy greenhouse gas or other kinds of energy to cool their food to eat at home. Also, when winter or summer is coming, families will choice either buy greenhouse gas or other kinds of energy to turn on heaters or air conditions when they feel too hot or too cold at home. So, it seems that future greenhouse gas will b some families' base essential energy choice product, due to green house gas does not make pollution to compare other kinds of energy and price is not very expensive when global any families choose to buy this kind of energy to use at home for long term benefit. However, future serious global warming climate environment changing effect will bring this question: Why will global warming climate changing factor cause global greenhouse gas energy consumers to choose other kinds of energies to replace it to use? I shall explain the reasons as below:

Some environment scientists had confirms that it has relationship between the possible supplying shortage challenge of the global greenhouse gas consumption level and the global climate warming growth. They indicates the required change in GHG emission intensity for each category, such as living need to use greenhouse gas to drive car, using greenhouse to cook food, (i.e. GHG emission per calorie, person kilometer of driving, square meter). The proposes concept provides guidence for any new greenhouse gas product developers, greenhouse gas consumers and government environment protection policymakers. Moreover, environment scientists indicated that we needs to protect our natural environment to avoid to cause air and water pollution due to our energy emission. They aim to reach the 2 degree climate target (2.1 tco2-eq. per capita in 2050 year. The GHG emission intensity of greenhouse gas consumption has to predicted to reduce by a factor of 5% in 2050 year.

They predict that future greenhouse gas will be applied to human's basic need, such as cooking food and driving car to work or entertain to be supplied to house energy consumers mainly. The reaching the GH intensity targets with future greenhouse gas product modifications, due to global climate warming environment changing negative influence, it will bring global greenhouse gas energy supplying shortage challenge causes and it will cause the greenhouse gas energy manufacturing cost to be raised and it will lead to change expensive greenhouse gas price to the kind of energy consumers. So, it will be possible to lead their needs for this kind of energy to be reduced, and they will choose to buy other kinds of gas to replace greenhouse gas to use for household energy consumers in the future. Hence, it seems that the greenhouse gas consumers number will be possible reduced ,due to the global climate warming is growing in the future.

In fact, human won't like global climate changes to more warm. Some climate scientists indicates when future global climate raises a long term temperature change of more than 7 degree above pre-industrial levels. Then, it will influence global energy nature resource supply number to be reduced and to supply to human to manufacture any kinds of greenhouse gas product (Meinshausen et al 2011).

Moreover , some greenhouse gas businessmen had considered the climate warming challenge will be possible to influence the greenhouse gas natural resource supplying number to be reduced to lead the greenhouse manufacturing cost to be raised. So, they had planned how to keep the greenhouse gas product manufacturing cost won't be raised to influence sale price to be raised to influence future home energy consumer number to be reduced. SO, some governments subsidize money to support greenhouse gas product manufacturers to encourage any kinds of greenhouse gas engineers to revise and innovate any new kinds of greenhouse gas product designs and consider how their efficient useful benefits to be continue consumed in order global home greenhouse gas users won't need to buy much greenhouse gas number to use if the new kinds of efficient useful greenhouse gas are invented by engineers. SO, it means that global greenhouse gas consumers can spend less money to buy the nowadays same number of greenhouse gas to use longer time , due to if future greenhouse gas can be used efficient to turn on cooking heater or turn on car engines or turn on heater, air conditioner machines to consume long time to use electricity for less electricity spending meter to compare nowadays electricity spending normal meter. Then, less electricity spending meter to use long time factor which can solve future greenhouse gas resource supply shortage challenge and energy consumers can spend the same money to buy same greenhouse gas nowadays number to use for longer time.

Hence, we need to wait future engineers' design innovation to invent new kinds of efficient useful greenhouse gas to replace nowadays non-efficient useful greenhouse gas product to benefit to future global home energy users to use. It implies the serious climate warming negative environment changing factor will raise future greenhouse gas consumer individual choice to buy this kind of natural energy product to use or it will influence their consumption desire to reduce to buy this kind of non-efficient useful greenhouse gas product, due to the warming climate caused the greenhouse gas natural manufacturing supply number shortage to lead cost raising and sale price will be raised in possible.

I recommend that U.S. any natural resource greenhouse gas product manufacturers need to concern how to design innovation to invent any kinds of efficient useful of greenhouse gas product to replace nowadays non-efficient useful greenhouse gas product before global climate warming is serious. If the future greenhouse gas efficiency use is exceed nowadays non-efficient use level of greenhouse gas, then future greenhouse gas consumers will feel it is worth when they can pay the same price to use longer time of greenhouse gas product. It will lead their greenhouse gas product consumption desires won't be reduced when global climate warming is caused in the future.

On the other hand, I shall explain how and why global population income level changing factor will influence future global greenhouse gas consumption desires to be reduced or raising. (Giro and De Haan 2010) explained to choose physical instead of monetary consumption per capital indicators since physical units are often easier to interpret are more directly related to environmental impacts and can capture saturation trends in consumption.

Hence, it s applied to greenhouse gas consumption case, if future global population income level is risen up. Then, it will encourage greenhouse gas consumption to be increased to every physical greenhouse gas number per capita for global every home energy user. Due to greenhouse gas is every family's essential energy product, who must need gas to turn on any cooker, air conditioners, heater to use at home or turn on car engines to drive cars on the road. So, it is global every energy home users' daily essential product. However, when global income level is increasing, it implies that global families green house gas consumption number will raise because when they have much money to save to buy food to cook at home often or they will often drive their cars to go to anywhere for entertainment or work or they often watch television or listen music or turn on air conditioners or heaters when they feel hot or cold at home. Then, they will spend much greenhouse gas to use to do any activities in home or sitting in car.

I shall bring this question: Why does global population income level raising , which will influence human's basic essential energy need to be raised as well as why can it influence greenhouse gas consumption to be raised? Some scientists explained these reasons as below:

When, human's income level raising, it influences human likes to spend more expenditure for travelling entertainment, e.g. many people like to spend much money to catch air plans to travel often. So, air planes will need much greenhouse gs to provide them to fly often.

Schafer et. al (2010) indicated that travel is commonly considered in transportation units of passenger distance (passenger kilometer). For GHG emissions, the modal split is also important. So, when global general population's income level is increasing, we will like to spend money for any travel entertainment. Any travel entertainment will need any transportation tools, e.g. high speed cars, public transportation, buses, trains, trams and air planes. All any one of these transportation tools which will increase to use greenhouse gas to provide to them to use. So, when global population's income level raising, we will often catch air planes to arrive different countries travel. When, we arrive the countries travel, we will catch the countries' trains, trams buses, ferries to travel in local. So, global any transportation tools will need to increase green house gas to use in order to satisfy global travelers' travelling entertainment needs. So, it explains why global transportation tools' greenhouse gas energy useful number will be increasing because when global population's income level is raising, then human will accept to spend more saving time to travel to different countries.

However, in any global travelers' journeys, they will need catch any transportation tools to go to anywhere to travel. So, increasing global traveler number, it will cause global transportation tools to use much greenhouse gas. Then, the greenhouse gas can be raised to charge global transportation service providers easily because global transportation service providers will need to buy much greenhouse gas to provide to them to drive.

Anyway, when global population income level is increasing, it will lead the greenhouse gas demand to be raised to global every home energy users' home energy need. For example, U.S. , Canada these both countries, their temperature will be below than 0 degree in winter. So, it will be very cold in winter. I shall suppose that when U.S. , Canada both countries' populations have high income level, then this high income level people have enough money to either turn on heaters often all day in order to keep their homes more warm and live more comfortable when winter is coming or they can turn on air conditioners often all day in order to keep their homes more cold and live more comfortable when summer is coming. So, the global greenhouse gas energy need will be increased when global the air conditioners and heaters are often turning on all days in winter or summer time.

Van Ruijven et al (2010) indicated that shelter can be described be floor space, which relates to live comfort as well as heating requirements. Hence, it explains why the global greenhouse gas need to global every family energy consumer number will be increased, when global population's income level is increasing. Because there are many people (different countries residents) in any countries, they like to spend saving money to raise their living of standard in their homes. So, any countries people (the country's residents) can accept to often turn on their air conditioners in home in order to let them feel more warm in summer, e.g. U.S. U.K. France, Germany. Also, any countries people (the country's residents) can accept to often turn on their heaters in home in order to let them feel more cold in winter, e.g. Hong Kong, Africa, China, Thailand. So, global warm will influence the climate change to either extreme hot or extreme cold temperature. When, global population income level is increasing, any country's home energy users will like to turn on their air conditioners or heaters to let their to feel comfortable when they are staying at home. So, it will influence the green house gas product consumption desire will be increased to global home energy users when the country is encountering extreme cold or hot temperature in the future.

Consequently, it explained that why global greenhouse gas product demand to public transportation tool service providers and home energy users will increase when global population income level is increasing as well as why global greenhouse gas product demand will decrease if global climate temperature is increasing , which will influence to global home energy consumers to decrease to buy any non-efficient useful greenhouse gas product when it's sale price will increase, due to cost is increased by greenhouse gas supplying number shortage challenge. Thus, it seems that they have indirect or direct relationship to influence future global greenhouse gas product's price changing and the greenhouse gas demand to home energy users and public transportation tool users. If any US greenhouse gas product manufacturers expected to sell their greenhouse gas product to global energy market in success. They need to plan how to invent efficient useful of new greenhouse gas product before the global climate warming factor influences.

● Will U.S. inequality of income factor influence long term greenhouse gas energy product consumer choosing desires to be reduced?

Finally, I shall give my opinions to explain whether how inequality of income factor will influence U.S. domestic natural energy, such as greenhouse gas product consumption desire to be fallen down if future U.S. economy encountered serious inequality of income in society.

On demand and supply theory explanation, it indicates that when the product supply is more thn market demand, then the product's price ought need to be fallen down in order to attract consumers to choose to buy it more to raise sale number in short time. Otherwise, when the product supply is less than market demand, then the product's price ought need to be raised because the product will be shortage to be supplied to sell to consumers to buy. It will have higher value, due to consumers worry about they can not buy the product later if they do not choose to buy the product immediately.

I shall apply this demand and supply theory to explain whether how U.S. domestic greenhouse gas product consumption market will be influenced when U.S had encountered serious inequality of social income economic changing in long term. Whether has it relationship between U.S. inequality of income and consumer's desire to purchase greenhouse gas energy product need?

In fact, greenhouse gas energy product will be U.S. home or family consumers daily essential energy consumption product. Because greenhouse gas product is one kind of non-pollution and clean energy to compare other kinds of power (energy) , such as petrol, oil. So, U.S. home or family consumers will prefer to choose to buy greenhouse gas to cook at home or us this kind of natural energy to replace other pollution energy, such as oil, petrol to drive their cars on the road in order to reduce air pollution in U.S. It seems that it will be future one kind of attractive environmental protection and non -pollution caused energy useful product. However, if it had enough greenhouse gas to supply in U.S. domestic energy consumption market and its price is reasonable. I believe that it can increase U.S. home (family) consumer numbers to choose to buy its energy product. Otherwise , if it had no enough greenhouse gas to supply in U.S. domestic energy consumption market and its price is not reasonable. Then, I believe that it can not increase U.S. home (family) consumer number to choose to buy greenhouse gas product easily. Although, it is one kind of non-pollution and clean energy product , but when it's price is not very reasonable to charge U.S. home (family) consumers. Then they can choose to buy the oil or petrol energy product to replace it if their price are more cheaper to compare greenhouse gas product in U.S. domestic energy consumption market. Due to U.S. energy consumption market has many different kinds of energy products to be supplied to U.S. home (family) energy consumers to choose. So, they won't worry about that they have none any kinds of gas to buy to cook at home or drive on road. Unless, U.S. domestic energy market has less number of energy suppliers or it is only greenhouse gas product supply, then it can attempt to raise it's sale price when the U.S. greenhouse gas providers ensure their supply number is less than U.S. greenhouse gas home (family) consumer demand number.

However, if future U.S. economic environment encountered serious inequality of influence or it won't influence U.S. domestic greenhouse gas energy consumption market. I shall give my opinions to explain as below:

What is inequality of income mean? Why will U.S. be possible income inequality? Is greenhouse gas product consumption in the U.S influenced by income inequality? In fact, in the case of United States, when income distribution has become more unequal since the 1990 year, the country's aggregate consumption growth has been maintained at a relatively high rate. However, Keynesian economists like Palley (2002) and Setterfield (2010) argue that the fast growth of aggregate consumption in U.S. can be attributed to an unsustainable is removed, the relationship between consumption and income inequality will be become obvious.

So, it seems that of U.S. 's debt financing is serious, then it will bring these bad influences , e.g. many U.S. people need to borrow money from banks for living, many U.S. businessmen need to borrow money for developing their business. Then, it implies that U.S. society has encountered inequality of income social problem. It will be caused possible that many U.S. people will be unemployed or the low income level of U.S worker number will be increased or their salaries or wages will be decreased. Them, they will not like to spend for entertainment, e.g. reducing travelling number or none of any travelling entertainment in every year. Then, it will be possible to influence the greenhouse gas demand to be reduced.

Why does it influence greenhouse gas demand to be reduced? For airline industry example, when U.S. domestic traveler number decreases, then the air plan flight number will also influenced to decrease, due to every year U.S. travelers reduce to spend money to travel because unemployment or low salary or reducing salary factors influence. It will lead air planes do not need to use more gas, such as greenhouse gas product to be energy to push their engines to fly often, such as any of long trip flying journey number will be reduced to fly to different countries and short trip flying journey number, such as U.S. domestic flying journeys will also reduced both. So, flight travelling flying number will be influenced to decrease and it bring air plans do not need lot of greenhouse gas energy to be supplied to them to fly. Hence, it is possible to impact airline industry to reduce to buy lot of greenhouse gas energy for flights needs, due to flight number is influenced to reduce from airline passenger number and flight flying number reducing factor.

On the other hand, U.S. inequality of income social problem will influence U.S. home (family) energy consumers do not need to buy lot of greenhouse gas product because many U.S. families won't often drive cars to go to anywhere in U.S. domestic travelling places for driving entertainment needs. Because U.S. inequality of income effect, it will influence many U.S. people face unemployment, reducing salary (wage) or when U.S. domestic economic environment is bad. U.S. government needs to borrow much money from overseas government to develop any technologic industry or different aspects of high knowledge industry development, e.g. artificial intelligence, space exploration mission. However, it has possible to increase greenhouse gas product need for space exploration industry, (AI) non-manual driving vehicle industry because these both industries will have needs to use greenhouse gas product to help their engineering to supply energy to carry on any experiment for their future new products sale market development.

In conclusion, it can explain that when U.S. society encounters inequality of income social challenge. It must not influence all U.S. consumer needs, such as (AI) non -manual driving vehicle manufacturers, space exploration rocket manufacturers both. They will still need any kinds of suitable greenhouse gas products to assist their non-manual driving vehicle engines or rocket engines to be supplies energy to implement their any future new products, such as (AI) non -manual driving vehicles, space exploration rockets product experiment needs. These both industry manufacturers' greenhouse gas product need , which won't be influenced to be decreased during U.S. is encountering bad economic environment causes inequality of income in society. Hence, U.S. inequality of income social challenge will only influence U.S. home (family) greenhouse gas product consumption desire needs and airline flight flying industry's greenhouse gas product desire needs to be reduced in possible, but it won't influence (AI) non-manual driving vehicle and space rocket manufacturers greenhouse gas product desire needs to be reduced because these both industries are high technological product development industry, they have market value to be carried on any experiments, so they must need lot of greenhouse gas to be used to implement any research experiments to satisfy future U.S. people space travelling or driving non-manual driving vehicles entertainment needs.

CHAPTER SIX

Long term trends in U.S. steel, aluminum, cooper mineral manufacturing consumption

I suppose that US big cities and small cities residents began to concern air pollution challenge. So, they will concern how their driving behaviors will influence air pollution when they often drive their cars to go to offices or any work places or entertainment places. So, air pollution factor will influence US big and small cities residents whether they ought choose to sell their cars or ought not buy any new cars in order to cause air pollution when they often drive their cars in big cities or small cities , US. So, this air pollution factor will influence future car need and sale number to be decreased, due to car sale decreasing number which will bring the needs of steel material to be used to manufacture any cars number is also decreased in big cities and small cities US. So, the steel need ought will be decreased , due to air pollution challenge in US.

Global steel mineral materials trends for global manufacturing industry is continue increasing needs to use steel, cooper, aluminum minerals to manufacture any products, e.g. car, boats, ships, furniture, machines, buildings etc. products. However, global any products for above these mineral materials manufacturers will select the most reasonable price and the best quality of any one these minerals to select to manufacture any products which need these mineral materials or component to produce. Hence, global mineral material (component) suppliers will trend to raise these any one of minerals to produce high quality products, long term durable, reasonable price sale demand to sell to consumers.

I shall give opinions to explain that how U.S. steel, aluminum, copper mineral component suppliers need to implement what kinds of sale strategy in order to attract global steel, aluminum, copper, mineral component consumers to select to buy their steel, aluminum, cooper mineral components more easily.

Firstly, I shall discuss iron or steel sector, since the iron and steel contributes considerably to industrial Co2 emission, it is important to identify the factors driving steel demand. Two major factors will determine future CO_2 emissions in the steel sector. The first is technological progress which could lead to more efficient production technologies. However, coal which is the main source of CO_2 emissions do not only serve as a fuel in the melting process and for casting and rolling the steel. Furthermore needed for the reduction of iron ore, which makes it difficult to trim down its use beyond a certain level, even if substantial progress has been made in corrective direction. So, advanced economies, such as developed country, U.S. any steel manufacturers can attempt to use coke to manufacturer steel more efficiently. Thus, technological process in steel making is one important factor which will drive the steel manufacture and sale industry's future CO_2 emissions. The other major factor driving CO_2 emissions from the steel sector is future global steel demand.

In past history , in the mid-1960 year, the industry reconstruction period, which led to an increase in steel demand and production. In this period, the advanced economies were the main drivers of global steel demand. So, new production techniques are needs to global steel manufacturers. Then 1990 year, the global steel demand began to grow when many products which need steel mineral component to manufacture. In fact, steel consumption demand growth depends on two factors as below:

The first considers the industry sector and its structure , it means whether how many products need steel mineral to be supplied to manufacturer. The second considers the country's income of its population and its demand for steel manufacturing products. Hence, any U.S. steel manufacturers need to consider what kinds of unique industries which are developing in the country in order to predict the country's steel demand more accurately. For example, China's car manufacturing industry needs many steel to manufacture cars. Hence, U.S. steel manufacturers can research what steel quality, shape, price are the most attraction to sell to China car manufacturers. So, as above explanation, high technological steel manufacturing method will be one important factor to influence future U.S. steel manufacturing industry export market in success. Due to other countries which have some steel sells and some steel manufacturers who can have high technology to manufacture steel , e.g. Germany is one successful steel manufacturing country because its steel manufacturing skill had reached mature stage. Hence, U.S. needs have advanced steel manufacturing technology to raise its steel quality to win its competitors.

Hence, nowadays, global steel manufacturing industry is increasing competition. Due to the relationship between steel use and per-capita income is close. Steel consumers (steel using product manufacturers) consider to measure of technological process how the steel manufacturers apply high technology to manufacture steel products. So, high technological steel manufacturing method will be one important factor to influence steel consumers (steel using product manufacturers, e.g. car manufacturer) to select to buy their steel products in nowadays global steel manufacturing industry. Hence, U.S. steel manufacturing factories need high technological equipment to help them to manufacture the best quality, the most long durable time steel products in order to attract global steel useful steel product manufacturers to select to buy U.S.'s steel products more easily.

On income hand, it concerns global steel useful product manufacturers' income (profit), it means that U.S. steel manufacturers need to know and evaluate whether how much profit past and future global steel useful manufacturer's product consumers (business clients) that they will earn or they had earned in order to predict whether how much steel number which they will buy. It is important reason to explain why U.S. steel manufacturers need to know how much profit their business clients will earn because the U.S. steel manufacturers can predict whom will be their next year clients. For example, if the country one steel mineral (component) useful product manufacturing client who had loss last year. it is possible that who will reduce to buy the U.S. steel manufacturer's steel product number to prepare to manufacture how much steel number is the most accurate because its client number is less to cause loss, even it won't need any steel need to prepare to manufacture more products, e.g. cars to raise sale. Otherwise, if the country one steel mineral (component) useful product manufacturing client who had profit last year, it is possible that who will increase to buy steel products number to prepare to raise many steel mineral manufacturing need of products, e.g. cars in order to satisfy many car clients' needs in possible. So, it is possible that they (the car manufacturers) need to buy much steel to prepare to manufacture their products in this year.

Conclusion, U.S. steel manufacturers need to evaluate global steel consumers or business clients whose past and present and future financial performance in order to predict how much steel number they will need to buy as well as they also need to raise steel manufacturing equipment efficiency and performance and quality in order to raise steel productivities and qualities to keep its long time durable useful value to satisfy every steel manufacturing products' consumer' needs, e.g. cars. Hence, these two factors will be future U.S. steel manufacturing suppliers who need to concern issue in order to attract global steel mineral (component) buyers' competitive good quality of steel products needs to achieve preferable selection to their U.S. steel products to buy in global steel competitive market.

Secondly, I shall indicate U.S. aluminum, cooper, mineral manufacturing industry is similar to steel mineral manufacturing industry, but they have different competitive sale strategy. I shall explain as below:

In the future, it will be how trends in consumption and global production to select minerals of cooper. Nowadays, to growth rate of primary production of aluminum and cooper. So, it causes threat to aluminum and cooper need for industry use, due to recycling technology can bring recycle re-use of aluminum and cooper nature to help industries to re-use any aluminum and cooper resources element to manufacture any products. So, the future trend of aluminum and cooper resources element will be reduced to global industries needs because recycling technology can bring cost benefits to let them to use recycling aluminum and cooper element. So, new aluminum and cooper resource element needs will be reduced.

Otherwise, the recycling re-used aluminum and cooper resources element has been re-used many times for the product manufacturers. Anyway, the manufacturers won't easier to select to buy new aluminum and cooper resource element. Although, the production of both primary and second recycled aluminum both have increased in fact speed. For most countries, there are no data to distinguish between production of secondary aluminum from past-consumer scrap (discarded aluminum products) and new (manufacturing) scrap. But, it seems, future trend of recycling secondary aluminum product demand is more than primary new aluminum product demand in global manufacturing industry market, such data indicated U.S. hich accounts for 50% of total world secondary aluminum product. So, it seems that secondary aluminum product (recycled) will be demanded more than primary new aluminum production. It also indicated U.S. 59% of the secondary aluminum was recovered from new scrap and 41% from post-consumer scrape. Hence, if implies future aluminum manufacturing industry consumers will select to buy secondary aluminum (recycling products) more than primary new aluminum non-used products. So, future trend in aluminum recycling product need will be reduced when nowadays aluminum resource element had been recycled to manufacture again new recycling elements many times to supply to global steel product manufacturers to re-use these nowadays recycling aluminum resource elements many times again.

I believe that future one day, when these nowadays secondary recycling aluminum resources elements had been used many times by global any product manufacturers. Then, they can be recycled to manufacture these old recycling aluminum resource element again. The effect will be that they can not be recycled to manufacture again because they had been recycled to manufactured many times. Their quality will be worst to compare primary (new) aluminum resource element to let global product manufacturers to use them to manufacture high quality of products to sell. So, I predict future primary new aluminum or cooper need will be increased because the second recycling aluminum or cooper resource element had been recycled to used to manufacture new products by different manufacturers many times. So, future the primary (new) aluminum or cooper need will be increased and price can also be influenced to be raised. Thus, I recommend that U.S. aluminum or cooper industrial manufacturing resource element manufacturers ought need to prepare how to seek new natural resource to manufacture primary (new) aluminum or cooper products and they ought not only concentrate on gathering reused aluminum or cooper to manufacture them again. Because , future global aluminum or cooper product consumers will prefer select to buy primary (new) aluminum or cooper more thn secondary recycling aluminum or cooper to help them to do any products to sell. So, future new (primary) aluminum or cooper product will be more proper to compare secondary recycling aluminum or cooper to steel in global industrial manufacturing market.

3.1 US lighting product consumption market characterization

I suppose that the US lighting product sale number has relationship to US future birth rate and young people population number. The reason is because that the big and small US cities students need to read books when they read books at homes at night after schools. So, if future US big and small cities have many young people who need to read books at night. Then, they must need often turn on lights to help them to read at homes. Then, this student consumers will bring every US big or small cities families need to buy many lights to use for their reading at homes. So, the future US birth rate will influence future student number. So, the big or small cities' young population will influence the lighting product sale number in future US lighting market. Every country has itself lighting market customer characterization because different lighting products have different types, functions, colors, designs to attract lighting customer choice. Lighting consumers functions include home reading room, dinner room, bed room, toilet function; office lighting working environment function; shopping center shopping environment functionl transportation tools driving at night etc. different light functions.

What are US lighting product unique characterizations? In US future lighting consumption market. Its lighting products will be focused on their unique advantages to beneficial any lighting consumers. US lighting product manufacturers will need to implement technological research such as: lighting energy saving technology. Energy saving is consumed by light sources in US, lighting technologies how many are installed, where they are installed, the performance attributes are of the installed stock of lighting technologies. So, future US lighting product is needed energy saving technology to help lighting consumers to reduce electricity expenditure at residential, commercial and industrial places for office, home, education, retail, public or private car driving light etc. different light needs. So, effective lighting energy saving technology will help public and business and personnel lighting users to reduce much electricity expenditure. So, lighting energy saving technology will be the most importnt factor to influence future potential light consumers to choose to buy the lighting product manufacturer's any lighting products to compare attractive design, style, shape, color , size light product appearance factors. Because in general, any lighting product consumers will like any lighting products can spend less electricity in order to reduce electricity expenditure when they use every day.

Hence, future US key elements of lighting product sale successful factor, any US lighting product sale market will need have these elements, such as: quantity, type, application, and energy use of stationary lighting in the

US. Performance characteristics of lighting technologies, trends, drivers and barriers to improved efficiency in the lighting market. Opportunities for energy savings through advances in lighting technology and adoption of best practices, overview of ongoing lighting research in the public and private sectors. It is not only only for lighting product sale in US domestic sale market. It is also included to lighting products export overseas market. Because global lighting product consumers consider how to consume less electricity to use lighting product in order to save electricity energy and expenditure. So, lighting energy -saving technology is value consideration to any US lighting product manufacturers in the future lighting sale market development.

Who will be US future energy -saving lighting product consumption target? I shall indicate as below: Residential consumption target can include manufactured residential , family manufactured business, lighting product consumer who needs lighting product to in their family factory, so they expect to spend less electricity for lighting expenditure in those family manufacturing proceed. Residential single family and multi-family either less than 4 units or 4 or more units, who needs lighting product when they have need to bath or eat dinner or read ot watch television any indoor activities when they are living in their residential homes at night. So, they also expect to buy energy- saving lighting products to reduce their electricity consumption expenditure. Another lighting product consumers are commercial lighting users. This commercial lighting consumer number will be large and their lighting electricity needs will also be much, due to they use light for commercial functions. Such as vacant, office/professional, laboratory, warehouse/non-refrigerated, food sales, public order/safety, health care (out patient) , warehouse (refrigerated), public assembly, religious worship, education, food service, health care (inpatient), hospital ward room patient light service, surgeon room medical surgeon light function , hotel/motel/dorm room light function, shopping mall/center light function for shopping customers, retail shops, excluding shopping mall lighting function etc. different commercial functions. So, lighting commercial customers number and their light needs will be more, due to commercial clients need to turn on lighting products in their stores or hospitals or warehouses etc. different indoor places to use in all days in possible.

Otherwise, residential family lighting users will only use light at night , due to who need to leave their homes to go to offices to work or go to schools to study. So, they will stay at house at night in common. Even, if they stay at homes in the morning or afternoon. They won't need to use lighting at this sunny time. So, residential light consumers will only use lighting product at night in common. Also, it will influence their demand of lighting products' design, color, energy -saving function. Their demand won't be very high. Otherwise, commercial lighting product consumers, they will often need light to help them to serve their clients or serve themselves in offices, hospitals, warehouses, schools, hotels, shopping malls (centers) etc. different places. So, this often useful functions influence their lighting products' design, type, color, what manufacturing material is used and the most important need is energy-saving demand, due to the light consumers can save more money to use lesser electricity. So, their lighting product demands are higher to compare residential lighting product consumers. This issue is US lighting product manufacturers need to consider before they decide how to manufacture any lighting products to sell to US domestic or export to overseas lighting market.

The final light consumer target is industrial consumption users. I believe that they will be the most need of light consumers. Because they will need light working environment to help their workers to work ot manufacture any products in factories. The industrial consumers include food product manufacturers, tobacco product manufacturers, textile mill product manufacturers , appear and other textile product manufacturers, apparel and other textile product manufacturers, lumber and wood product manufacturers, furniture and fixtures product manufacturers, paper and allied product manufacturers, printing and publishing product manufacturers, chemicals and allied product manufacturers, petroleum and coal product manufacturers, rubber and miscellaneous plastics product manufacturers, leather and store, glass product manufacturers , primary metal industries manufacturers, fabricated metal product manufacturers, industrial machinery and equipment product manufacturers , electronic and electric equipment manufacturers, transportation equipment manufacturers. Due to they need many workers to help them to manufacture any products in factories. So, enough light environment is important to influence their productivities and efficiencies. So , they will need to buy many lighting products to assist their workers to work anywhere in factories. So, anywhere in factories will need much light to let workers to feel comfortable and viable. So, this industrial light consumers target will be the lighting product's main consumers because they must need to buy many lighting products to let their workers to work in enough light factory environment, even if any lighting products are damaged or used to long time, they will buy other better quality new lighting products to replace these any one of damaged or old lighting products.

In conclusion, it seems that industrial lighting customer number ought be the highest and their demand to lighting products' light quality , such as reducing the lowest dark environment, energy-saving function, lighting products' safety and lighting products' durable and even reasonable price demand which will be the most top to compare other kinds of lighting product consumers in US , even overseas export lighting market. All US lighting manufacturers ought need to concern how to design the attractive different kinds of lighting product styles to satisfy these different kinds of lighting product consumers' needs, instead of design aspect, energy-saving technology, light color, size, reasonable price etc. different factors will influence lighting consumer number.

CHAPTER SEVEN

Prediction future global fruit and vegetable soft drink consumption behavioral trend

I suppose that future US big and small cities young, adult and old people began to concern health issue. So, they need to buy fresh fruit, food , e.g. pork, beef, sheep , vegetable to eat. It will bring the fresh fruit and food need to be increased. in US big and small cities. Due to these are essential food to every US people. So, supermarket businesses can choose to build their supermarkets to locate offices, schools entertainment places in cities, they ought not build their supermarkets in country , e.g. near farming location. Because food consumers will not be farmer target consumer. They will be students, working people in cities mainly. So, future supermarket choice will influence food consumer number in US big and small cities.

State of the plate (2015) indicated that the U.S. fruit and vegetable consumption market trend after a brief rise through 2005 year, US per capita fruit and vegetable consumption has declined 7% over the past five years, this has been driven primarily by decreased consumption of vegetables (-7%) and fruit juice (-14%). If fruit juice is excluded from the overall fruit total. However, these is only a 2% decrease in fruit consumption over the past 5 year. So, fruit has seen growth among certain subsets of the population, specifically children of all ages and adult ages 18 to 44 age.

Hence, it seems that fruit juice is popular to be selected to drink for children and young, adult consumers in U.S. food market. Otherwise, U.S. consumers can select either to buy fresh fruit and vegetable to eat or buy fruit juice and vegetable juice to drink in U.S. fruit and vegetable health food market. However, U.S. food consumers will have possible to decrease fruit and/or vegetable soft drink consumption. The factors include ongoing interest in consuming low-carbohydrate foods, which peaked a decade ago, and the ever-increasing competitive set of beverages available to consumers that include flavored water. So, U.S. fruit or vegetable soft drink consumers will have possible to reduce fruit or vegetable soft drink consumption because they feel flavored water beverages or fresh fruit and vegetable will be low-carbohydrate food. Otherwise, fruit and vegetables soft drink are " sugar-sweetened" beverages. It will give less health to compare fresh fruit or vegetable food.

Why is fruit or vegetable food the main food to U.S. people daily? The reasons include that : In U.S. eating habit, fruit has enjoyed gains in U.S. people traditional consumption habit t breakfast. This is likely because breakfast is a more health related meal and fruit. For example, berries and bananas have gained favor all day, probably due to their versatility for consumption and these both fruits are as a topping for cereal or yogurt or as an ingredient to a smoothie or hot cereal.

Future global children and young and adult and old age food consumers whether they will change their eating habit to accept fruit and vegetable soft drink to replace fresh fruit and vegetable food more easily. I believe that every different age fruit and vegetable food consumer targets who will have different food need. For old age fruit and vegetable food consumer target , U.S. fruit and vegetable soft drink manufacturers need to persuade old age fruit and vegetable consumers to change their fresh fruit and vegetable food eating habit for better medical conditions , it is as a category to bring stronger health benefit to persuade higher consumption rates among older consumers. Global many old age people are concerning their health and greater incidence of medical conditions.

In specially, for the consumer ages 50 or above. Their eating habits are usually to select fresh fruit and vegetable to eat. So , it is more difficult to change their eating habits to select fruit and vegetable soft drink more easily. Unless, U.S. fruit and vegetable soft drink manufacturers can find some strong points which can influence global old people feel fruit and vegetable are not meeting in terms of their health and daily lives. Other influential factors which will be possible to influence their food and fruit habit changing to select fruit and vegetable for their daily lives need, e.g. reasonable price, better taste, shopping convenience. For example, yogurt is a natural gaining for fruit or vegetable and some fruit can work well on pizza or a variety of vegetables can be included on poultry sandwiches. All of these complementary food groups are also among the fastest growing food items. They can have much competitive effort to influence global traditional fresh fruit and vegetable consumers to select to buy these kinds of complementary fruit and vegetable to eat sometimes in daily lives because they can provide fresh taste of food choice, due to their taste will have some different feeling to let global fresh fruit and vegetable consumers to fee when they are eating. Also, choice of anywhere locations to sell fruit and/or vegetable soft drink, this factor is also important. In retail, these has been a lot of focus on the perimeter of the store, but the center of the fruit and vegetable soft drink store location is important and fruit and vegetable soft drink or natural drink for fruit product or vegetables and some fruit pizza or a variety of vegetables include on sandwiches which can be sold on different countries' cities restaurants or food retail shops or pizza retail stores which can be selected to locate to any country's central cities in order to attract travelers or working people to find these restaurants conveniently to buy different kinds of manual manufacturing of fruit and/or vegetable taste of soft drink or food restaurants to drink or eat for breakfast, lunch or dinner.

In conclusion, the future global future fruit and vegetable soft drink consumption influential factors will include taste, retail location choice, drink or food element manufacturing factor in order to attract global fresh fruit or fresh vegetable food consumers' consideration If U.S. fruit and vegetable soft drink food manufacturers expect to change global fruit and vegetable food consumers' traditional eating habits easily. They must have good sale plans for how to maufacture attractive taste, how to select suitable locations to sell and how to charge the price to let global different fruit and vegetable food consumers to feel their fruit and vegetable soft drink products are more reasonable price to compare traditional fresh fruit and vegetable food. However, fruit and vegetable will have possible to be not fresh when they are saved long time in any stores or farms location. Otherwise, fruit and vegetable soft drink will have long time to save to ice box to wait to drink. So, it is maunal manufacturing of fruit and vegetable soft drink food product's stronger point to compete to natural fruit and vegetable food.

4.1 Prediction U.S. future global daily food
industry trend

The research and insights committee indicated that it discovered U.S. daily food industry had no longer significant increases in gross domestic product and population expansion to drive domestic growth. So, it brings this challenge for U.S. daily food product manufacturers' cost savings / gains driven and production efficiencies will be possible caused to U.S. daily food product caused to U.S. daily food product manufacturers in domestic market. So, they ought consider how to expand overseas daily food product market to attempt to increase more different kinds of daily products to different countries. I shall recommend some solutions as below:

U.S. daily food product manufacturers ought plan future five to ten year opportunities to drive the growth of daily / daily -based food products to overseas different countries. For example, Hong Kong, China, Japan Asia countries have many people who like to buy U.S. daily food to eat or drink, e.g. milk, cheese, ice-cream. So, they need have good identification of macro trends and a greater understanding of data-based key elements (e.g. the country's demographic shifts, prediction of the country has how many people who like to eat or drink any kinds of daily food, e.g. Japan's one city Tokyo has how many people who like to eat or drink any kinds of U.S. daily food ; finding every country's people whose food / eating behaviors, e.g. in what situation which will influence Japanese have desire to buy daily food, such as the consumption group , e.g. prediction of young or old age Japanese number will like to eat or drink U.S. daily food in what time of one day for the old or young age Japanese eating habit, e.g. morning time, lunch time or dinner time. So, the U.S. daily food manufacturers can follow the suitable time to prepare sell the accurate number to Japan. For example, if they predict there are 500,000 about Japanese young and old age people who like to buy U.S. daily food to eat or drink after dinner time in Tokyo city every week. Then, they can export enough different kinds of daily food number to Tokyo every week ; retail channel shift , e.g. supermarket or small retail store ; food service promotion perspective , .e.g. newspaper or magazine or radio daily food service promotion channel choice to let the country people to know what kinds of U.S. daily food can be sole to the country. Then, these methods can help any U.S. daily food manufacturers have potential to predict the accurate consumption number to every countries and U.S. itself to raise their daily food export or local sale number.

These methods aim to investigate whether what kinds of daily food products sale to the country's people who will be accepted to buy to eat or drink more. For example, how many Japanese are living in the city , e.g. Tokyo , who like to buy milk, daily beverages, cheeses, yogurt, frozen daily and daily is as an ingredient or a component food to eat or drink. Thus, market research can help the U.S. daily food manufacturers to attempt to predict every export country's different cities daily food product buyer number and predict what kinds of daily food will be popular to choose to eat or drink for the country's different cities' peoples' eating culture or habit. So, U.S. daily food manufacturers need have a leading global strategic planning to predict future how consumer insights and trends will how and why and when change in order to make more accurate daily food customer behavioral predictive analysis to satisfy the country's daily food product consumer need and making the more accurate suitable population daily food sale distribution for different kinds of daily food products to the country.

The daily food market research strategic plan will be marked by increasing rates of change driven by key macro forces as below:

Firstly, U.S. daily food manufacturers need to evaluate uncertainty over policies, economy, supply and different kinds of daily food prices will be possible to increase traditional middle income Americans and global daily food consumer number. It depends on their brands whether are familiar to their daily food consumers because U.S. daily food industry will need to evaluate how global market environment economic changes and daily food product supply is predicted to the different kinds of sale number and global daily food product consumer's demand in order to measure the most accurate sale price to different kinds of daily food to let global daily food consumers to feel the brand of daily food suppliers' sale prices are more reasonable in order to raise its consumer number and define the both low-end (social reasonable acceptance of premium sale price strategy) in global competitive daily food market.

Secondly, U.S, daily food manufacturers need to innovate or improve their manufacturing method to raise different kinds of daily food products' qualities, improving daily food product formulation , e.g. taste, health food elements, attractive daily food and consumer beneficial package and advertising doctors' medical health confirmation message offerings to let global daily food consumers to know. Due to nowadays, global (including U.S.) daily food product consumer number will be increasingly diverse and more globally aware (aging population, growing and extending to a more diverse youth demographic daily food product consumer trend). The changing face and resultant health conditions of global daily food product consumers will require daily food as well as brands of different kinds of daily health food products' food health quality will be needed to raise in order to satisfy their health food needs.

Finally, smart shopping technology will be increasing demand to U.S. different brands of daily food manufacturers. Global health daily food consumers will choose to buy any kinds of daily food from digital technology, i.e. online shopping is one kind of fast long distance point of purchase decision making capabilities. Also, smart shopping technology will alter and raise global daily food product consumers' health food expectations of retail to more of an experience. So, how to select sale channels to buy the brand's daily health food which will be one important factor to influence every brand of daily food product manufacturer in success because global daily food product consumers had been influenced by internet only shopping channel. For example, U.S. some daily food consumer who are living far away from cities, if their home locations has no any supermarkets, and they need to drive long time to arrive the locations where have supermarkets. Then, they need to choose to buy any kinds of daily food products from internet because daily food product price is cheap and purchase number is less. So, they will compare the journey of their gas spending needed to drive their cars and driving time from homes to supermarkets as well as internet online shopping channel.

Usually, if U.S. daily food product consumers will prefer to choose to buy these kinds of daily food from internet channel when they need to drive cars to go o supermarkets. The reasons is because that they can earn more economic benefits of less time and less cost from internet online shopping channel to compare driving cars to go to supermarkets channel to buy the only daily food product every time. For example, their daily food today sale product include, yogurt, cheese, freeze food etc. these kinds of daily food products which are the most popular to buy from internet online channel for the living far away supermarkets to satisfy lower order convenience needs for internet online shopping channel. This reason is supported on behavioral economic theory to explain why internet online shopping channel is more acceptance to the living far away from supermarkets.

In conclusion, any brands of U.S. daily food product manufacturers ought consider these above any strategies in order to raise their competitive effort in global daily food product market in success more easily.

4.2 Prediction U.S. future alcohol, wine
consumption trend

Nowadays, some economists predicted U.S. to be the largest wine, alcohol the largest drinking consumer. What are the factors cause U.S. has effort to be grown demand in global wine or alcohol industry. I shall follow the global economic changing factors to estimate how and why global wine consumers' behaviors are influenced to choose to buy U.S. wine or alcohol by global economic changing factor influences.

One reason is found evidence which is based on wine or alcohol quantify determinants of global wine consumption influence. It seems that U.S. every year wine or alcohol manufacturing number will influence global wine or global consumers why to choose U.S. wine or alcohol to drink. I shall explain why economic factor will influence U.S. wine supply number. For example, when the year, it has oversupply of grapes to import to U.S. for wine manufacturers to manufacture and kinds of wine drinking products, which made possible the introduction of extreme value wines in U.S. country.

When the global economic environment is good, many people has jobs to work. Then, it will cause many people consider to choose to buy the better quality of different kinds of wine to drink, due to global many people have extra money to save. They have effort to spend to drink at lest one bottle better quality of wine to drink. Thus, the global wine drinker number will increase. With the rise in per capita income in U.S. itself country and other countries as well as the year oversupply of grapes import number can be supplies to let U.S. any wine manufacturers to manufacture different kinds of better quality wine in order to sell to overseas and U.S. domestic wine drinkers. Thus, in the year, the demand for higher quality food and beverages , e.g. wine is expected to rise , due to the year economic environment is good and U.S. oversupply number of grape to prepare to manufacture different kinds of better quality wine in order to satisfy global high quality wine drinkers' taste needs.

Hence, it proves that global economic environment changing factor and U.S. better quality of wine supply factor will influence U.S. wine drinker number. If the year economic environment is bad, global many people lose jobs and the farming growth environment is poor, it has not good climate to grow many grapes to rise their number for U.S. wine manufacturers to manufacture any kinds of wine products. Then, U.S. wine supply number and global better quality of wine drinker number both will decrease. Thus, global economic environment and U.S. better quality of wine drinkers' demand will have direct or indirect relationship to influence U.S. wine sale number.

Other U.S. wine export number successful factor considers U.S. wine manufacturers ought consider different countries' wine drinkers' taste , reasonable sale price demand and their drinking wine culture (drinking habit). Historically, U.S. wineries adopter either of three methods to sell any kinds of wines drinking product. They include lifestyle, product or production. I shall explain as below;

Firstly, lifestyle means tht every country's wine consumers will have themselves wine drinking culture or habit to choose which kinds of wine or alcohol drinking product to drink. So, if any U.S. wine drink product manufacturers can know the country's wine consumers' preferable wine product choice.

Then, they can evaluate whether which kinds of wine product to decide to sell to the country more accurate and easily, product of wine. It means that they can know how to produce high quality wine products, e.g. using how much grapes or lemons or oranges or apples etc. fruit element and sugar and how to keep the suitable temperature to save every bottle of wine in wine stores in whole wine manufacturing procedure efficiently in order to manufacture the best taste of different kinds of fruit wine to sell to the different countries' target consumers to sell. Because different countries' wine consumers who have different taste preferable needs and wine qualities and drinking culture (habit) needs. So, they need to gather data concerns different countries' wine drinking consumers' preferable choice needs in order to choose the best suitable kinds of wine taste to sell to the country proper to drink.

Finally, it is production cost aspect, it concerns how much costs of every kind wine to manufacture every kind of wine products. It is very important to influence every U.S. wine suppliers' consumer number because if it's production cost, e.g. finished wine product lorry transportation cost in U.S. domestic places between the wine manufacturer's factory and wine stores or fruit transportation farming places and its wine manufacturer's factory which transportation cost is high as well as overseas air plane fruit transportation cost to be delivered the wine manufacturer's factory or the U.S. finished wine products are needed to transport to overseas wine market to sell to different countries' air plane freight cost which is high, then these transportation cost will influence the U.S. wine seller's sale price to be raised if it needs often to deliver any wine finished products to overseas or domestic win both markets. Then, the U.S. wine manufacturers' high delivery behavioral cost will impact to global wine consumers' desires to be fallen down because they will feel its sale price is not too reasonable high to reduce their wine consumption desires.

In conclusion, these three aspects of factors, which are every U.S. wine drinking product manufacturers need to consider before they achieve to do any kinds of wine businesses.

The other research considers U.S. alcohol consumption in U.S. and overseas markets. Alcohol is different to wine because some people feel alcohol, e.g. beer . It can hurt human's health, when the alcohol drinker often drinks beer. Otherwise, wine is health drinking product to global drinking consumers' feeling usually. So, U.S. alcohol manufacturers' consumers target will be limited to sell to the people who do not worry about any kinds of alcohol product , e.g. beer which can but to their health. Unless, U.S. alcohol manufacturers can being good message to change the alcohol drinking consumers' attitudes to feel any alcohol products won't hurt whose health. Hence, U.S. alcohol manufacturers need have good methods to let global alcohol drinking consumers change to drink alcohol attitudes to let them to feel alcohol won't influence their health when they sometimes or often drink alcohol.

Hence, how to change their drinking alcohol habit to be accepted to drink alcohol behaviors which won't bring hurt to influence their health , this changing of drinking alcohol habit or attitude issue which will help any U.S. alcohol manufacturers to increase alcohol consumer number in long term. So, it is one valuable researching matter to any U.S. alcohol manufacturers. Moreover, it is valuable to understand the trends and possible future patterns for alcohol consumption by beverage type given that the consumption of some alcoholic beverage types trends to have more strongly relationship with outcomes or actions that increase externality costs and negative health outcomes.

Also, U.S. alcohol manufacturers need to consider that every country's government charges how much alcohol taxes to import countries' alcohol manufacturers because any U.S. alcohol manufacturers will choose to raise higher alcohol sale price if the country government needs them to charge higher alcohol taxes to import t the country. Then, it will bring negative emotion influence to the high alcohol import tax country's alcohol consumers, due to the U.S. alcohol manufacturers charge higher sale price to their different kinds of alcohol products immediately. The sudden alcohol raising price factor will influence the high alcohol imported tax country's alcohol consumers feel any kinds of U.S. alcohol products won't be one kind of health drinking product, due to their sale prices are raised suddenly. They will consume to drink the kinds of U.S. drinking products, e.g. fruit juice, wine to replace U.S. alcohol drinking products. So, any U.S. similar alcohol taste products will be the export alcohol drinking product manufacturers' competitors if the U.S. alcohol manufacturer's one alcohol imported country plans to raise 10 to 20%, even more alcohol imported tax to their alcohol products next month. Then, the imported alcohol country's alcohol consumer number will be caused to reduce more easily. Hence, any U.S. alcohol manufacturers need to consider when the import alcohol countries will raise alcohol imported tax to charge them in order to select other low alcohol imported tax or no raising imported tax countries to increase to export more alcohol products to them to replace the high tax countries alcohol imported to keep their competitive effort and build good brand to the U.S. alcohol manufacturers' image to the high alcohol imported tax countries' alcohol consumers to let them to feel the brand of U.S. alcohol manufacturer's alcohol is still valuable to select to buy to drink.

4.3 Factors influence US tea, sugar, orange and pork food export

US tea consumption strategies

U.S. has different kinds consumption taste of tea drinking product to be grown by farmers. Then, some of tea will be chosen to sell to U.S. domestic market as well as some of tea will be chosen to export to U.S. overseas market. I shall explain what factors will influence U.S. tea export and domestic tea sale number and suggest methods how to avoid their sale number to be influence reduced.

In fact, global tea demand is elastic, so any factors will influence global tea consumption more easily if some factors influence its change, when they have direct or indirect relationship. I shall indicate several factors will be easily to influence demand of tea, they may include traditional price variable tea , and tea consumer income variable factor, demo graphics such as the country general tea consumers' age, education, occupation and cultural background factor.

Some U.S. tea professionals analyzed that the most influential U.S. tea market factors will the consumers' income and tea's prices both factors, then another factor will be the country's demographic factor when they have small change, they will bring relatively small impact on U.S. tea consumption. I shall indicate the methods to solve these challenges as below:

What is comprehensive demand system method. This method would cover both complements and substitutes for tea, demographic characteristics for each of the major market, e.g. the major tea market includes China, India, Japan, UK, US itself country . Then, U.S. tea manufacturers can know what can be these countries' substitutes and the countries' the consumers' demographic characteristics, then it can evaluate the reasonable tea retail prices to let the major tea export countries' consumers to feel more acceptance when the substitutes for tea supply number will increase or their price will reduce , in order to avoid to lose many tea consumers when their preferences to buy and choose these any kinds of tea substitutes products.

The analysis was therefore restricted to three products of the beverages group, namely black tea, green tea and coffee. These kinds of tea product will be the most popular tea drinks. So, US tea manufacturers can concentrate on manufacturing more different taste for these three kinds of teas as well as making budget how much expenditures to spend to manufacture the number of these three kinds of tea products of the major tea consumption countries market. For example, India is one tea popular drinking country. Indian like to drink black tea, green tea and coffee. However, India has other kind of similar tea taste substitutes to let Indian to choose tea product. So, US tea manufacturers need to consider whether how much retail prices are the reasonable for India tea substitutes products and how much number and kinds of the similar tea substitutes to compete to US any brands of tea manufacturers. So, India tea market research is needed to gather data similar taste substitutes before the US brand of tea manufacturer selects to export how many tea number and kinds of tea taste to India. The data includes the demand elastic of India tea consumer, e.g. evaluate how much the retail price for black tea green tree and coffee and evaluate how much number of black tea, green tea and coffee to supply to India in order to avoid the India tea consumers choose to buy other similar tea taste substitutes if the US brand of tea retail price is too high to let them to feel not reasonable price to choose to buy its teas to drink. So, US brand of tea manufacturers also need to find which kinds of tea similar taste drinking products will be its substitutes in order to evaluate how much black green, green tea, and coffee price is the suitable to attract them to choose to buy its these kinds of tea to drink.

US sugar consumption strategies

Sugar must be global food consumers' essential food product. For home consumers who must need to buy sugar to cook food to raise better taste or mix water to drink. For food manufacturers who must nee to buy sugar to manufacture any foods to sell to their food consumers. So, US sugar manufacturers' sugar target consumers will be global different countries food consumers. But, it also have different countries' sugar competitors, due to many countries have sugar manufacturers which have natural resources to supply to manufacture different kinds of sugar, e.g. white sugar, yellow sugar, coffee sugar and cooking sugar etc. to sell in global market. So, US sugar manufacturers need have goof sugar sale strategies in order to win global sugar competitors.

Sugar market strategy will focus on the supply and demand of refined sugar and their main determinants of quantified. For example, how to select the best sugar market or countries to sell among global different countries, finding what factors can affect the production of refined sugar, as of the main supply of sugar element as well as an analysis of the world price of sugar, as one of the well as how to analysis of the world price of sugar, as one of the significant factors affecting the world sugar market.

In fact, it has direct relationship influence between the world sugar market in agricultural and good production . If the sugar supply number is less to the country, then the country food manufacturers won't have enough sugar supply in order to make any kinds of food. So, the US sugar manufacturers can apply sugar demand and supply strategy to evaluate how much sugar number to supply to the country to sell and as well as evaluate how much sugar price charge to the country manufacturers in order to raise the maximum sugar profit. So, it needs to gather data consider the country has how many food manufacturers need to buy sugar to make any kinds of food in order to predict the accurate enough sugar supply number won't be exceed too much to the suitable supply demand to the country different brands of food manufacturers who need to use sugar to manufacture their food to sell in order to avoid too much sugar supply or too less sugar supply to cause their sugar sale price can not achieve the highest level. For the country sugar consumers, the US sugar manufacturer can also apply demand and supply strategy to raise sugar price. For example, it can gather the country's different brands of sugar competitors' sugar price data and sale number. Then, it can conclude the more accurate market sugar sale price level and sugar sale number in order to evaluate how much big of sugar export number and every big of sugar number and every big of sugar weight, e.g. how many sale bag number of five kg sugar or 10 kg sugar number the each big sugar sale price is the most reasonable sugar supply number and sale price to sell to the country home sugar consumers. Hence, market research strategy is one important factor to influence the US sugar supplier exports to the sugar demand country's consumer in success.

US orange consumption market strategy

Finally, I shall discuss the characteristics of US orange consumption market. In general, orange is a kind of health fruit to let human to eat. So, every country will have many people will prefer to select to buy orange fruit to eat.

In fact, US is one main orange export country. It will export its orange to Japan, Hong Kong, China, India etc. different countries. So, its orange market will have potential to develop and expand to different overseas markets, due to global the number of selection orange fruit eating people had been increasing seriously. However, how to keep its orange market competitive effort to win its competitors, it is one valuable consideration issue to any brand of US orange suppliers because Japan, China etc. Asia countries which have also different orange suppliers to sell their orange to overseas and domestic sale. So, the orange market competition is also serious. Also, it implies the US orange suppliers need have good sale strategies to solve this competitive challenge. I shall indicate some sale strategies as below:

(USDA) indicates that oranges fruit are the most consumed fruit in America. The orange is a favorite fruit among Americans. It has consistently ranked as the third most consumed fresh fruit behind bananas and apples. As a juice, it ranks number one. O average, Americans consume 2 and half times more orange juice annually than its nearest competitor apple juice. According to the per capita disappearance data complied by the U.S. Department of Agriculture's (USDA).

Economic research service (ERS), it showed that fresh orange consumption declined 36% between 1959/1960 year and 2000/01 year. Nowadays, fresh consumption appears to have peaked in the 1950 and 1960 year. When production was growing and consumers relied heavily on fresh products for most of their fruit consumption average about 19 pounds per person annually. After declining in the 1970 year through the early 1990 year to about 12 pounds annually fresh orange consumption now appear to be making a comeback.

Americans are increasing their consumption of fresh oranges which are mixed other fresh fruit and vegetables as a mean of a healthy diet. Other large number growing supply cheap sale price beneficial factor which is caused by bigger crops in recent years have made fresh oranges more available number supply and less experience, further driving up orange consumption demand in U.S. Also with bigger crops, increased import of oranges and apples, grapes etc. different fruits especially have increased suppliers and alternatives available to U.S. and overseas consumers for U.S. orange export industry development.

Other orange fruit supplement product is orange juice, which had increased orange consumption long term time and it is also one kind of substitutes product to influence the decline in consumption of fresh oranges when fresh orange consumers choose to drink orange juice because consumers feel to drink orange juice , which can substitute fresh orange consumption to receive many of the same health benefits. However, the demand of orange juice can influence the orange supply number. For example, as price consumption rises, the demand for orange increased , due to the greater quantity of fruit needed to make a single serving of orange juice versus eating one fruit orange on average, it takes one pound of oranges to make one 8 ounce glass of single strength orange juice.

It caused the demand of US orange production has grown 2% per year since the 1960 year. Hence, if these two countries people , e.g. Hong Kong, China have many people select to drink lot of orange juice. It means that these two countries people seem they have many people like to drink orange juices more than eat oranges. Then, it will need to increase many pound of oranges to manufacture many orange juices. Also, it will cause many fresh oranges will need to be used to manufacture orange juices. So, it will bring one challenge such as: How to keep the fresh orange and orange juice enough supply number to satisfy Hong Kong and China fresh orange juice and fresh orange fruit consumers in order to avoid shortage orange supply or shortage orange juice supply to export to these both countries for any US orange juice or orange fruit suppliers.

It is one valuable orange supply question to US orange suppliers consideration. I shall recommend that one predictive sale method to solve this shortage oranges or orange juices supply challenge. Such as this shortage fruit orange or orange juice to export to Hong Kong, China case, I recommend that any US orange juice and orange fresh fruit suppliers who can gather China and Hong Kong different cities population data and past year every cities orange purchase number or orange juice purchase number to predict how much will be their next year orange demand need and orange juice demand need number. Hence, they can follow every cities' predictive fresh orange fruit or orange juice number to be more accurate judgement to manufacture the predictive need of orange juice number or keep the enough number of fresh orange sale number in order to avoid the shortage of fresh orange fruit or orange juice supply challenge to China and Hong Kong both cities. For example, if the one city China , Shanghai had 9 million people. It was predicted 2 million people like to drink orange juices and 3 million people like to eat fresh oranges. But the US orange supplier has only 2 million oranges.

Hence, it must select to either to use all orange to manufacture orange juices or select to sell all fresh oranges only. Hence, when the country people has exceed orange or orange juice demand to have the US orange supplier needs to manufacture how to sell orange or orange juice number decision. However, I think the best sale method is that the orange supplier can select to sell 1 million fresh oranges fruit as well as it can select to use another 1 million oranges to manufacture orange juices. So, the US orange supplier's all orange supplier can sell this 2 million orange number to satisfy the China , Shanghai city fresh orange fruit and fresh orange juice fruit food consumers' needs.. It won't influence either all Shanghai city people have none any the brand of US oranges to eat, if all these oranges are needed to manufacture orange juices to supply to them to drink on they have only the brand of US fresh oranges to eat, if none of them are used to manufacture fresh orange juices to supply to them to drink in the year. So, the best orange or orange juice sale strategy to any country, it is half orange and half orange juice sale number in order to satisfy the country's fresh orange and fresh orange juice consumers' needs. It is one valuable question , which concerns how to arrange the reasonable orange and orange juice sale number to satisfy any country's consumer question to every US orange suppliers.

Factors influence US pork consumption

Nowadays, pork ranks third in annual US meat consumption, behind beef and children averaging 51 pounds per person. US pork consumption varies by race and ethnitity. In general, US blacks race people consume 63 pounds of pork per person per year, whites race people 49 pounds and Hispanics 45 pounds. Otherwise, higher income US consumers tend to consume less pork.

Demographic data in the CSFII suggest future declines in per capita pork consumption, as increases of Hispanics and the elderly in US , who eat less port than the national average, enlarge their shared of the population. However, total US pork consumption will grow because of an expansion of the US population, e.g. US immigrants number will increase from different overseas.

In fact, although pork isn't consumed by certain populations or certain regions, it is one of the preferred meats in the world and United States. So, understanding the basic factor underlying pork consumption will help US to supply in pork market and will able the meat industry to as well as it well the enable the industry (Economic research service, 2004).

In conclusion, US pork high income and white race consumers do not prefer to select pork to eat. it is possible due to they feel port is most common meat and purchase easily food. Hence, pork manufacturer (suppliers) ought raise pork sale quality and better taste, e.g. upgrade common pork from low meat quality and poor taste class meat to raise to high meat quality and better taste class meat to compare beef and sheep meet substitutes. Hence, building good public image to pork that is very important to influence US pork domestic consumption market, even overseas markets. This issue is all US pork suppliers need to consider if they expect to raise pork meat consumption effort in success in long term future.

CHAPTER EIGHT

Factors influence US tourism consumer behavior

I suppose US big cities have many high education and high income residents are living. So, their foreign tourism entertainment needs will increase and they will choose long travelling days journey and they will choose foreign tourism more than domestic tourism because they can spend more money to go to overseas for long time travelling. Otherwise, US small cities have many low education and low income resident are living. So, their domestic tourism entertainment needs will increase and they will choose short travelling days journey and they will choose domestic tourism more than foreign tourism because they can not spend more money to go to overseas for long time travelling.

Nowadays, tourism industry is every country's main leisure income. Every country will need have itself unique tourism features to attract travelers to go to travel easily. So, attractive unique tourism features can persuade different countries travelers choose to go to itself country to travel more easily. I shall recommend what factors can influence global travelling consumers choose to go to US travel more easily. The travelling strategies can attempt to be implemented as below:

Firstly, US tourism leisure providers (travel agents) need to know what different countries' tourism consumers why and how to persuade them to feel US anywhere places are valuable to go to travel, what can attract them in these places, for Chinese travelers case example, what Chinese like to play when they choose to go to any one of the US domestic travelling places. So, the US tourism leisure providers need to define the Chinese tourism consumers' tourism acts, attitude and travelling decisions regarding choosing, buying and consuming tourism products and tourism services and also its past consumer tourism reaction. Due to different countries' tourism consumers who have different tourism leisure needs, e.g. Chinese young age travelers prefer to choose to tourism package arrangement, who only like to buy air tickets and arrange their travelling journeys, e.g. they can choose where they will live and anywhere they choose to travel. So, US tourism service providers only concentrate on introducing anywhere US places valuable to let them to travel, calculating every journey transportation cost, and living and eating cost to let Chinese young tourism consumers to know. Otherwise, Chinese old age tourism consumers prefer to the US tourism service providers can arrange whole tourism journey to help them to reduce their worries about paying how much rent to live hotels, transportation costs in US anywhere journeys. Due to US is a large area country, many Chinese will feel worry about how to catch the bus, ferry, domestic air place, taxi, train , tram etc. transportation to go to any US domestic tourism places to pay the cheaper cost as well as how to find the reasonable price of hotels to live as well as how to choose the most valuable travelling places to travel and US anywhere tourism places can be exciting and comfortable and enjoyable tourism leisure feeling in their whole US tourism journeys.

In special, the Chinese old age tourism consumers must consider above these challenges, they must need the US tourism leisure provider ensures to help them to arrange all their US tourism journey needs, then they will reduce worry to choose who is the best tourism leisure service provider if the US travel service provider can solve above all challenges for their US domestic journeys. So, the US domestic tourism leisure arrangement service market competition is serious. Every US domestic tourism leisure provider needs have unique travelling leisure arrangement to attract them.

Secondly, US tourism service providers need to attempt to find different countries' tourism consumers' tourism leisure needs and how they make travelling journey decision processes because it can assist marketing manger to improve his/her own decision making process to forecast future different countries' tourism consumers' behaviors and to have a real and objective image of the country's general tourism consumer tourism leisure and tourism journey arrangement demands.

Hence, US tourism leisure service providers need to spend time to gather past different countries' tourism journeys arrangement tourism experience to develop new tourism products and services . It will include these questions for each country's travelling consumers' demands, such as below:

Who is important in the whole travelling journey arrangement decision making final tourism consumer?

What are the criteria every family or friend travelling group consumers' choice based on? e.g. travelling journey cost includes hotel, food, air ticket, leisure activities expenditure or how many days of the whole travelling journey criteria.

Where or when do they buy air ticket?

All these criteria will influence every tourism group consumer to make final travelling decision making to choose the US travelling service provider or another one. Hence, when predicting travelling consumers buying processes, sometimes the travelling service provider will make false assumptions about these processes can result in an wrong assumption. Otherwise, good tourism journey arrangement product or service is not being bought. But, every time of making false assumption will raise the more accurate judgement effort to predict future every country's travelling consumers' journeys' arrangement and improve their travelling journey arrangement skill when their every time of false assumption. Hence, every US travel service provider won't need to fear fail to make false assumption. Otherwise, they need to revise every time false assumption in order to improve next time travelling journey arrangement service quality in order to raise their satisfactory level.

Thirdly, US travelling service providers need to understand what the factors can influence overseas travelling consumers' behavior. The factors include the personal factor, such as tourist's personality, self image, attitudes, motivations, perceptions, life style, age, family life style, profession. For example, if the travelling consultant felt the tourist, he/she likes to contact exciting things, then he/her travelling leisure will be the exciting travelling destinations, e.g. Walt Disney theme park, climbing mountain sport, riding bicycles on hill sport, swimming sport, catching fast speed train transportation tool tourism journey arrangement. Otherwise, if the travelling consultant felt the tourist, he/she likes to contact quiet things, then his/her travelling leisure will be the quiet travelling destinations, e.g. walking around shopping centers, visiting book shops , walking on beaches etc. US cities or countryside walking travelling journey arrangement.

The another factor concerns the country's social culture, family, social class, reference groups. For example, Japanese social culture is common high social class to compare Chinese, Indian etc. So, their travelling demand will be higher to compare Chinese and Indian. For example, they like to eat better taste of food, when they choose to go to anywhere to travel. So, US travelers need to arrange the better taste of food to eat. However, whether the US journey which have arrange Japan restaurant or Indian restaurant or Chinese restaurant to provide Japan food or Chinese food or India food taste to these countries travelers to eat. It is very important to influence any countries tourism consumers to choose to go to US to travel.

The other factor concerns situational factor, such as time, psychology, ambiance, social ambiance, state of mind. The country's good or bad social culture can influence travelling consumption motivation attitude. For example, when the country had good social culture to encourage the country's people to spend money to travel easily. So, this kind unconscious or conscious motivations are encouraged by the social culture to its living people. Then, its living people will be encouraged to select, organize and interpret sensory stimulation into a meaningful tourism picture of the world. So the country's good travelling leisure social culture will encourage the country's people to accept to spend money to go to anywhere for travelling leisure easily. It is one social tourism culture to encourage the country people to spend money to travel when they have holidays. So, any US tourism leisure service providers need to know what the country's social culture is in order to select the most suitable travelling destinations to attract them to travel to themselves America country more easily.

The other factor concerns age which is an effective discriminator of tourism consumer behavior. For example, young travelers have every different tourism tastes as regards travelling products or travelling trip service arrangement to compare to old travelers. Also, young age travelers tend to spend more than old age travelers. Thus, if the travelling service provider can predict what travelling needs of the old or young age traveler segments which can rise interest in tourism marketing from those tourism behavior point of view are: childhood , teenage, first youth, second youth and old age different tourism age segments' unique tourism leisure arrangement and tourism service and evaluate whether the travelling package price is the most reasonable to satisfy their different tourism age segments needs in order to evaluate the most reasonable travelling package price charge. Moreover, profession also has a great impact on tourism consumer behavior, profession young or old tourism segment and non-profession young or old tourism segment, due to their education level has high or low difference. So, its impact over an individual tourism decision is obvious difference. For example, professional young or old age travelers can have more money to spend high class expensive tourism leisure. So, tourism journey arrangement can be belonged to a medium or high class. They usually demand high rates accommodation and meal and expensive train, air plane, ferry etc. transport tools in their auxiliary services during the journey. Otherwise, non-professional young or old age travelers can not have enough money to spend high class expensive tourism leisure. So , tourism journey arrangement can be belonged to a low class. They usually demand low rates accommodation and meal and cheap tram, train , air plane, ferry etc. transportation tools in their poor services during the journey.

Thus, US tourism firms will need have interest in attracting opinion leader because their abilities to influence groups and try to convince them regarding the tourism service quality of their tourism service needs.

The final factor concerns economic factor. It is the most sensitive to environmental change and it is as a result, US tourism service providers have been very affected by the global economic situation influence.

In the past, tourism plays an important role in the European economy. Many labor were dominated by this tourism industry, due to global number of visitors has been increasing fast in the past between ten to twenty years. Thus, the global economy is influenced to recovery, being influenced by economies from Asia and America which register continued and considerable increases.

As Europe tourism industry case, many countries implemented domestic tourism visitor number measures, delaying the economic recovery perspectives, already weak. The euro and American dollar, but the possibilities tourist from all over the world, with of special offers and low price vacations. Thus, economic factor influences dollar exchange change which will also influence global travelers choose whether they ought need choose Asia or Europe or America to travel by exchange dollar variable factor influence.

Hence, US tourism leisure service providers need to concern global economic environment how will change in order to make solutions to avoid global travelers choose to go to Asia or Europe or America to travel, due to these countries' money exchange rate can bring beneficial to let them to spend less than choice to go to US travel. So, it implies that economic changing behavior can influence global tourism consumers to choose to go to America to travel, even their earlier tourism country is US.

In conclusion, all these factors will influence global travelers' tourism countries choices and tourism leisure activities and tourism journey arrangement choices serious. Thus, US tourism leisure providers need to consider global economy will how change and discover many different kinds of tourism leisure arrangement package in order to arrange the different kinds of the most suitable tourism leisure package to satisfy global tourism consumers' unique tourism leisure consumer segments' needs.

Reference

Economic research service, factors affecting US pork consumption, 2004

Economic research service, USDA ,U.S. Department Of Agriculture Economic Research Service (ERS)

Girod, B. and De Haan P 2010 More or letter ? A model for changes in household greenhouse gas emissions due to higher income J. Indust. Ecol. 14 31-49.

Meinshauen M et al 2011. The RCP greenhouse gas concentrations and their extensions from 1765 to 2300 clim._change 109 213-41.

Palley Thomas I. 2002 " Economic contradictions coming home to roost? Does the U.S. economy face a long-term aggregate demand generation problem? Journal of post Keynesian Economics, Fall 2002, vol. 25 no. 19

Setterfield , mark, 2010, " Real wages , aggregate demand and the macroeconomic travails of the U.S. economy. Diagnosis and prognosis. " Trinity college department of economic working paper 10-05.

State of the plate , 2015. study on America's consumption of fruit and vegetables, product for better helth foundation, U.S.

Van Ruijven B. De Vries B. Van Vuuren DP and Van Der Sluijs, JP 2010 . A global model for residential energy use: uncertainty in calibration to regional data energy 35 269-82.

How applying economy theories solve US consumer market behaviors

CHAPTER NINE

How applying economy theories solve US consumer market behaviors

In service market, we can apply demand and supply theory to solve some service market consumer behaviors.The economic problem – sometimes called the basic or central economic problem – asserts that an economy's finite resources are insufficient to satisfy all human wants and needs. Economics involves the study of how to allocate resources in conditions of scarcity However, viewing economics as the study of how society allocates resources can lead to conflation of normative economic planning and empirical study of how economic agents operate in these conditions.

In mainstream neoclassical economics, it is assumed that humans pursue their self-interest, and that the market mechanism best satisfies the various wants different individuals might have. These wants are often divided into individual wants (which depend on the individual's preferences and purchasing power parity) and collective wants (which are the wants of entire groups of people). Things such as food and clothing can be classified as either wants or needs, depending on what type and how often a good is requested.

However, economists have sometimes characterized "how" to produce as a "technological problem" of efficiency whereas the allocation of what is produced is an "economic problem". In a free market, the "how" of production and allocation of resources is distributed among economic agents. In a centrally planned economy, a principal decides how and what to produce on behalf of agents. Modern economies are often welfare capitalist with various regulations, which makes the economic system more equitable while retaining the distributed free market system. Due to human wants are unlimited, an infinite series of human wants remains continue with human life. Nobody can claim that all of his wants have been satisfied and he has no need to satisfy any further want. Everybody feels hunger at a time then other he needs water. Sometime one feels the desire of clothing then starts to feel the desire of having good conveyance. When all existing wants are satisfied then new wants starts to create in mind, so the series of wants remains continue till the last moment of life. So an economic problem arises because of existence of unlimited human wants.

● Problem of allocation of resources

The problem of allocation of resources arises due to the scarcity of resources, and refers to the question of which wants should be satisfied and which should be left unsatisfied. In other words, what to produce and how much to produce. More production of a good implies more resources required for the production of that good, and resources are scarce. These two facts together mean that, if a society decides to increase production of some good, it has to withdraw some resources from the production of other goods. In other words, more production of a desired commodity can be made possible only by reducing the quantity of resources used in the production of other goods.

The problem of allocation deals with the question of whether to produce capital goods or consumer goods. If the community decides to produce capital goods, resources must be withdrawn from the production of consumer goods. In the long run, however, [investment] in capital goods augments the production of consumer goods. Thus, both capital and consumer goods are important. The problem is determining the optimal production ratio between the two.

In fact, in our societies, resources are scarce and it is important to use them as efficiently as possible. Thus, it is essential to know if the production and distribution of national product made by an economy is maximally efficient. The production becomes efficient only if the productive resources are utilized in such a way that any reallocation does not produce more of one good without reducing the output of any other good. In other words, efficient distribution means that redistributing goods cannot make anyone better off without making someone else worse off. (See Pareto efficiency.) So, scientists will apply efficient distribution methods to help any countries to earn the absolute advantages when we buy and sell any kinds of products or food between ourselves countries, e.g. when US has good natural resource to grow any food, e.g. potato, wheat , vegetable, cotton , then US can export to sell to China, because China has no any farms to grow agriculture food to supply itself Chinese to eat. So, China must need to buy any agriculture food from US. Otherwise, China has cheap labor to supply to US any manufacturers to help them to manufacture their electronic products. SO, it has many US factories are built in China to let Chinese workers help them to produce their products because their wages are cheaper to compare US workers. So, comparative economic advantage will be choice to apply between US and China both countries. (Absolute advantage trade theory)

The inefficiencies of production and distribution exist in all types of economies. The welfare of the people can be increased if these inefficiencies are ruled out. Some cost must be incurred to remove these inefficiencies. If the cost of removing these inefficiencies of production and distribution is more than the gain, then it is not worthwhile to remove them.

● The problem of full employment of resources

In view of how to use available resources are fully utilized is an important one. A community should achieve maximum satisfaction by using the scarce resources in the best possible manner—not wasting resources or using them inefficiently. There are two types of employment of resources:

(1) Labour-intensive

(2) Capital-intensive

In capitalist economies, however, available resources are not fully used. In times of depression, many people want to work but can't find employment. It supposes that the scarce resources are not fully utilized in a capitalistic economy.

● The problem of economic growth

If productive capacity grows, an economy can produce progressively more goods, which raises the standard of living. The increase in productive capacity of an economy is called economic growth. There are various factors affecting economic growth. The problems of economic growth have been discussed by numerous growth models, including the Harrod-Domar model, the neoclassical growth models of Solow and Swan, and the Cambridge growth models of Kaldor and Joan Robinson. This part of the economic problem is studied in the economies of development.

● Needs and wants problems

Needs are things or material items of peoples need for survival, such as food, clothing, housing, and water. Everyone has a different needs and wants. Until the Industrial Revolution, the vast majority of the world's population struggled for access to basic human needs.

Wants are effective desires for a particular product, or for something that can only be obtained by working for it. While the fundamental needs of survival are key in the function of the economy, wants are the driving force that stimulates demand for goods and services. To curb the economic problem, economists must classify the nature and different wants of consumers, as well as prioritize wants and organize production to satisfy as many wants as possible.

● Five bases problems of economy

In our societies , in general, our societies will have these similar problems The following points highlight the five basic problems of an economy. The problems are: 1. What to Produce and in What Quantities? 2. How to Produce these Goods? 3. For whom is the Goods Produced? 4. How Efficiently are the Resources being utilized? 5. Is the Economy Growing?.

Problem 1:What to Produce and in What Quantities?

The first central problem of an economy is to decide what goods and services are to be produced and in what quantities. This involves allocation of scarce resources in relation to the composition of total output in the economy. Since resources are scarce, the society has to decide about the goods to be produced: wheat, cloth, roads, television, power, buildings, and so on. Once the nature of goods to be produced is decided, then their quantities are to be decided. How many tones of wheat, how many televisions, how many million of power, how many buildings, etc. Since the resources of the economy are scarce, the problem of the nature of goods and their quantities has to be decided on the basis of priorities or preferences of the society.

If the society gives priority to the production of more consumer goods now, it will have less in the future. A higher priority on capital goods implies less consumer goods now and more in the future. But since resources are scarce, if some goods are produced in larger quantities, some other goods will have to be produced in smaller quantities. Suppose the economy produces capital goods and consumer goods. In deciding the total output of the economy, the society has to choose that combination of capital goods and consumer goods which is in keeping with its resources.

Problem 2: How to Produce these Goods?

The next basic problem of an economy is to decide about the techniques or methods to be used in order to produce the required goods. This problem is primarily dependent upon the availability of resources within the economy. If land is available in abundance, it may have extensive cultivation. If land is scarce, intensive methods of cultivation may be used. If labour is in abundance, it may use labour- intensive techniques; while in the case of labour shortage, capital-intensive techniques may be used.

The technique to be used also depends upon the type and quantity of goods to be produced. For producing capital goods and large outputs, complicated and expensive machines and techniques are required. On the other hand, simple consumer goods and small outputs require small and less expensive machines and comparatively simple techniques.

Further, it has to be decided what goods and services are to be produced in the public sector and what goods and services in the private sector. But in choosing between different methods of production, those methods should be adopted which bring about an efficient allocation of resources and increase the overall productivity in the economy.

Problem 3. For whom is the Goods Produced?

The third basic problem to be decided is the allocation of goods among the members of the society. The allocation of basic consumer goods or necessities and luxuries comforts and among the household takes place on the basis of among the distribution of national income. Whosoever possesses the means to buy the goods may have then. A rich person may have a large share of the luxuries goods, and a poor person may have more quantities of the basic consumer goods he needs.

Problem 4: How Efficiently are the Resources being Utilised?

This is one of the important basic problems of an economy because having made the three earlier decisions, the society has to see whether the resources it owns are being utilized fully or not. In case the resources of the economy are lying idle, it has to find out ways and means to utilize them fully.

Problem 5: Is the Economy Growing?

The last and the most important problem is to find out whether the economy is growing through time or is it stagnant. If the economy is stagnant at any point inside the production possibility curve, it has to be moved on to the production possibility curve PP whereby the economy now produces larger quantities of consumer goods and capital goods. Economic growth takes place through a higher rate of capital formation which consists of replacing existing capital goods with new and more productive ones by adopting more efficient production techniques or through innovations.

All of these economy problems will be our societies often causes to anyone feels need to solve problems in order to achieve our societies can have enough resources to satisfy our every day living.

● The Consumer Problem

Consumer theory is concerned with how a rational consumer would make consumption decisions. What makes this problem worthy of separate study, apart from the general problem of choice theory, is its particular structure that allows us to derive economically meaningful results. The structure arises because the consumer's choice sets are assumed to be defined by certain prices and the consumer's income or wealth. The consumer's problem is to choose that is most preferred or, equivalently, that has the greatest utility.

The assumption of perfect information is built deeply into the formulation of this choice problem, just as it is in the underlying choice theory. Some alternative models treat the consumer as rational but uncertain about the products, for example how a particular food will taste or a how well a cleaning product will perform. Some goods may be experience goods which the consumer can best learn about by trying ("experiencing") the good. In that case, the consumer might want to buy some now and decide later whether to buy more. That situation would need a different formulation. Similarly, if the agent thinks that high price goods are more likely to perform in a satisfactory way, that, too, would suggest quite a different formulation. Agents are price-takers. The agent takes prices p as known, fixed and exogenous. This assumption excludes things like searching for better prices or bargaining for a discount.

Hence , it seems that economic problems and consumer problems are similar, I feel that it is possible , economists can attempt to apply any economic theories to solve some consumer problems in some situations. They can find the accurate solutions when they can apply the suitable economic theories to solve the suitable consumer or economic problems in our societies. I shall indicate that how economists can apply the suitable economic theories to attempt to solve some consumer problems in our societies as below:

Demand And Supply Theory Solves Consumer Problems

What is economy rule predict consumer behaviour? Why and How does economist can apply economy rule to predict consumer behaviours? I shall explain the reasons as below:

Why does economic principle be the best to predict consumer behaviour. It may include these two reasons: The first focuses on the substantive domain of study, in this interpretation , economics is a social science devoted to understanding how the economy works. The second definition focuses on methods: economics is a way of doing social science, using particular tools. In this interpretation the discipline is associated with formal modelling and statistical analysis rather than particular hypotheses or theories about the economy. Therefore, economic methods can be applied to many other areas besides the economy, everything from decisions within the family to questions about political institutions.

● Demand and supply principle predict public transport tool passenger behaviour

Economists need to use the right economic ideas to predict consumer behaviour. So, Misuse the wrong economy ideas to predict consumer behaviours. It will do more wrong judgement to evaluate or predict why and how and when the country's consumer behaviours will change. It is every economist needs to consider issue. For example, the economy idea application of economic supply-demand principles to public transport. Different fares would give commuters with more-flexible hours the incentive to avoid peak travel times. They would allow passenger traffic to spread out over time, reducing the pressure on the public transport system when enabling even larger total passenger flow. IT aims to reduce traffic congestion, increased public-transport use, reduced car-bon emissions and cause air pollution and generated considerable revenue for the country's transport system. So, if the country can apply supply and demand economic principle to attempt to predict how many passengers number needs to catch transport tools to go to work or go to school or other activities. Then, it can predict how many bus, ferry, taxi, train, underground train, tram etc. different public transport tools to satisfy future public transport passengers' needs in society. So, this demand and supply principle is the comparative best rule to predict any kinds of public transport passengers' road needs, when they need to either go to school, go to office, go to leisure or shopping etc. different kinds of activities. So, applying the demand and supply principle to predict road and sea public transport passengers can help the country to reduce air pollution when they feel that they can find any public transport tools to catch any time conveniently , then it can encourage them to reduce car purchase desire. When many people choose to catch public transport tools, then it will reduce many cars number on the road. Then, air pollution will reduce as well as any public transport tools' income will also increase as well as traffic jam will also reduce. When the country can evaluate how many people choose to catch bus or taxi or ferry or train or underground train, or tram or train etc. different kinds of public transport tools, then the country can predict the more accurate public transport tools number to every kind of public transport tool to satisfy their journey needs. e.g. whether underground train or train or tram need to decrease or increase the frequent times or number to catch the volume of passenger in busy or non-busy time; or whether bus company has need to increase how much buses to catch the city location passengers when they are living in the city. Moreover, supply and demand principle can help any public transport tools to explain why their passengers number reduces in the year, it may due to fare charge is unreasonable, feeling uncomfortable to sit on the seat or air condition is poor in the transport tool environment, or there are no more seats because many there are much time is full passenger and no seat vacancy to provide to them to sit . So, supply and demand principle can help any kinds of public transport tools to find whether which is (are) the factor(S) can influence the current or last year passengers number reduce. Then, they can concentrate on improving their weaknesses to raise their service quality . So, supply and demand principle can also help they to evaluate whether what their weakness are in order to improve to increase passengers number. They can do questionnaires to enquiry their passengers' response to evaluate whether which areas of services that they feel unsatisfactory. So, the different kinds of service satisfactory feeling to the passengers number data will be the main source to help the kind of public transport tool to analyse and conclude the results more accurate, then they can make the more accurate judgement to improve the of service. For example, the questionnaires indicate that the many passengers feel the bus fare is reasonable, but many passengers feel they can not find any seats to sit easily. So, it implies that the bus firm ought buy more buses or enlarges bus size and increases more seats in the enlarged buses. Then, it does not reduce its fare but it needs to find solutions to let passengers can find seats to sit in every bus more easily. But, if the questionnaires indicate that there are many passengers feel its fare is higher or unreasonable to compare other kinds of public transportation tools. Hence, it can avoid to spend more expenditure to increase bus number to the city, if the city has many passengers , they still choose bus to catch, but they feel its fare is too higher to compare other kinds of public transport tool. Then, it only needs to reduce its fare , it ought help it to increase passengers number. Hence, demand and supply principle is the most suitable economic method to evaluate any kinds of public transport system passenger needs in any country nowadays.

● Supply and demand and price elasticities principle predict oil energy user behaviour

The another case is that demand and supply principle can predict oil buyer behaviour to find whether what factors can cause the oil buyer individual need reduces. For example , a rise in production costs increases market prices and reduces quantities demanded and supplied. Or when, energy cost rise, utility bills increases and households fid extra ways of saving heating and electricity. But, others are nor. For example, whether a tax is imposed on the producers or consumer of a commodity, say oil has nothing to do with who ends up paying for it. The tax might be administered on oil companies, but it might be consumers who really pay for it through higher prices at the pump. Or the extra cost might be imposed on consumers in the form of a sale tax, but the oil companies might be forces to absorb it through lower prices. It all depends on the " price elasticities" of demand and supply. With the addition of extra assumption, this model also generates rather strong implications about how well markets work. In particular, a competitive market economy is efficient in the sense that it is impossible to improve one person's well-being without reducing somebody.

● Demand and supply principle can misuse to predict consumer behaviour when the two firms participate advertisement to promote their products in the same time

Why can demand and supply principle misuse to predict consumer behaviour when the two firms participate advertisement to promote their products in the same time ? I shall explain as below: Assume that two competing firms must decide whether to have a big advertising budget. Advertising would allow one firm to steal some of the other's customers.

But when they both advertise, the effects on customer demand cancel out. The firms end up having spent money needlessly.

We might expect that neither firm would choose to spend much on advertising, but the model shows that this logic is off base. When the firms make their choices independently and they care only about their own profits, each one has an incentive to advertise, regardless of what the other firm does. When the other firm does not advertise, you can steal customers from it if you do advertise, when the other firm does advertise, you have to advertise to prevent loss of customers. So, these two firms end up in a bad equilibrium in which both have to waste resources. This market can not apply demand and supply principle to predict consumer behaviours because they depends advertisement to promote their products. If these two firms advertise their products in the same time. Then , it is not possible that if one firm increases it price and it will cause its customer number loss, due to its advertise can help it to attract customers to consider its product from television or radio or newspapers or magazine promotion channels. So, I suppose that these two firms decide to increase their price, when they advertise their products to let customers to know in the same time. They will not lose their customers or reduce their customers easily. Because their customers can be persuaded to choose to buy their products to compare other similar products in preference. So, their increasing price will not influence their customers number lose easily. It explains that demand and supply principle is not right to this case, so demand and supply principle can misuse to help them to predict consumer behaviours when they advertise their products in the same time. Also, demand and supply principle is not suitable to them to predict consumer behaviours when they advertise their products in the same time. They will do wrong prediction to their consumers purchase desire when they advertise their products in the same time.

ON conclusion, using these demand and supply and price elasticity techniques, economists derive specific prediction for how consumers choose which products to buy, how households save, how firms invest, how workers search for jobs, as well as for how these actions depend on the particulars. They can help them to predict job and consumption behaviours more accurate, it depends on whether the situation is right, such as both competition firms participate to advertise their products in the same time case, it is not right to apply above economic principle to predict consumer behaviours. They will get wrong prediction when they apply this principle to predict consumer behaviours.

However, demand and supply principle can predict below any one of these cases. I shall indicate as below:

The problem of need-based scholarships: Most systems for providing college scholarships are based on some definition of financial needs, with scholarships generally being given only to those students who must need financial help in order to attend school.

Is need, rather than academic ability, the best basic on which to choose those students who are to be encouraged to attend college? Which way of choosing who gets aids is the more just? Which is the more efficient ? Is the overall educational level of society increased more by giving financial aid to bright students or to needy students? Presumably the aid offers more leverage to needy students, since they all need the money in order to attend college, whereas, many of the bright students would attend college in any case. But is a smaller number of bright students the more important addition?

So, the school can apply demand and supply principle to predict whether how many parents feel need financial assistance and evaluate how much financial amount is the right to borrow. It aims to calculate how many parents feel real financial need and how much to lend to them in order to let these students to get the most fair financial assistance.

Assuming the school wish to use need as a basis, how does the school determines " financial need"?

Is need a function or parents' income? What, then , does the school about children of wealthy parents who are living independently of them and get no aid from parents? Should they be punished for their parents' wealth? But if they are given aid, won't all students, in order to get aid, claim to be independent of their parents?

Is need solely a matter of family income, or should not the school takes a family's financial obligations into account? Does not it make more sense to give aid to someone whose parents must put night more children through school than to someone from a family of five or one only with the same income? But in a possible parallel situations, should a family that carries mortgages on one or two large homes get preference simply because they do not have much money left to spend on college? Does doing this reward ? Is there a difference between the case of night children and the case of the large mortgage? How should parents who are not married , but are living together and supporting their children jointly be counted? Most parents are supporter to their children , although they are married in possible.

So, the school needs to gather all these data to evaluate how many parents are not married or married or living with their children together, how much salary they earn as well as every family has how much children as well as whether they have mortgage for their houses. So, these number will be the financial education assistance demanders, but it does not represent their real financial needs. It is possible that someone does not feel any financial need, although their children apply financial assistance to your school. Then , your school needs to evaluate whether how much financial assistance can lend to every real financial need student family. It can not exceed your final financial expenditure budget (supply) , when your financial expenditure is not enough. SO, demand and supply principle can be applied to research this school real family financial demand to lend to the real financial need families and evaluate whether the reasonable financial amount to lend to every child family to study in your school.

● Supply and demand principle applies to immigration to decide wage case

A fascinating and important example of supply and demand, full of complexities, is the role of immigration in determining wages. If you ask people , they are likely to tell you that immigration into California or Florida US, surely lowers the wages of people in those regions. It is just supply and demand analysis of immigration. According to this analysis, of these to these two regions in US. Immigration in to a region shifts the supply curve for labor to the right and pushes down wages. Why has it relationship between immigration to US these two regions immigrant number and wage?

Careful economic studies cast doubt on this simple proposition, however, a recent survey of the evidence concludes:

The effect of immigration on the labor market outcomes of natives is small in US. There is no evidence of economically significant reductions in native employment. Most analysis, finds that a 10 percent increase in the fraction of immigrants in the population reduced native wages by a most 1%.

How can we explain the small impact of immigration on wages? The main mistake is to forget how mobile the American population is and that the impact of immigration on wages, we must examine the effect of new immigrants when the strength of the local economy and the number of native-born residents in a city are unchanged, that is , when these other things are held constant. Unless you exclude the effects other changing variables, you can not accurately predict the impact of immigration. The same principle holds in doing a supply0and demand analysis of any market. As much as possible, when you are examining the impact of a supply or demand shift, you must try to keep all other things constant.

● Rationing by prices

By determining the equilibrium prices and quantities of all inputs and outputs, the market allocated or rations out the scare goods of the society among the possible uses. Who does the rationing? A planning board? Congress or the president? BO, the marketplace, through the interaction of supply and demand, doe the rationing. This is rationing by the purse.

What foods are produces? This is answered by the signals of the market price. High oil prices stimulates oil production, whereas low food prices drive resources out of agriculture. Those who have the most dollars votes have the greatest influences on what goods are produced. All of these considers how demand and supply to the market.

For whom are goods produces? The power of the pursue indicates the distribution of income and consumption. Those with higher incomes end up with larger houses, more clothing, and linger vacations. When the most urgently felt needs get fulfilled through the demand curve.

Even, the how question is decided by supply and demand. When corn prices are low, it is not profitable for farmers to use expensive tractors and irrigation systems, and only the best land is cultivated. When oil prices are high, oil companies drill in deep offshore waters and employ novel seismic techniques to find oil.

IN sum , any thing needs through demands, interact with costs of goods, as reflected in supplies in our economic world. Hence, demand and supply theory ought be the most accurate method to help any businesses or governments to predict their shareholders behaviours when they will change as well as how and how their behaviours change.

Consumer choice theory solves consumer problems

What is 'consumer choice theory'?

'Consumer choice theory' is a hypothesis about why people buy things. Put simply, it says that you choose to buy the things that give you the greatest satisfaction, while keeping within your budget. At the heart of this theory are three assumptions about human nature.[1]

The first assumption is that when you shop, you choose to buy things based on calculated decisions about what will make you happiest. In economics language, this is known as utility maximisation (Economists really like to put quite simple concepts into long complicated terms.)

Secondly, the theory assumes that no matter how much you shop, you will never be completely satisfied. In other words, you will always be happier consuming a little bit more. This is known as the principle of non-satiation. Thirdly, even though you always get more happiness from more consumption, the amount of pleasure you get from each good decreases with the more you consume. So if you eat two ice creams rather than one, you get more overall pleasure, but the second ice-cream won't be as satisfying as the first. This is known as decreasing marginal utility.

Consumer choice theory has influenced everything from government policy to corporate advertising to academia. But the theory has been criticized for not being the most accurate description of how people actually make choices. A whole new branch of economics, called 'behavioral economics', has emerged essentially to use findings from psychology to disprove the assumptions behind consumer choice theory. This has also led others to argue that consumer choice theory is less about describing how we do actually behave, and is more about describing how people should behave.[3] In other words, by portraying people as self-interested shopaholics, economists are saying that is it okay and natural for us to be avid consumers.

● Consumer choice theory can be applied to solve consumer problems during the country can have economic growth , the reasons may include as below:

The scenario leading to inflation starts with poor growth. Forget about everything that comes next and focus on that most important factor. Because it happens that the scenario leading to a budget crisis also starts with poor growth, and the scenario leading to a long-term unemployment crisis starts with poor growth, and a scenario leading to a better-the-neighbor trade crisis starts with poor growth, and so on. So a very important question is: what can be done to improve the prospects for economic growth? In particular, what is the right countercyclical approach to take to best situate the economy for future growth? I shall indicate during US, America's economy growth occurs, then economists can attempt to apply customer choice theory to solve US itself country's consumer problems more easier.

In no small part, the question comes down to interpretations of charts like the one at right. On the one hand, long and deep downturns seem to have almost no effect on the long-term rate of growth. On the other hand, in the long run we're all dead, and those who live during an extended period of economic weakness suffer for it. Meanwhile, it's also difficult to see where high debt levels influence the long-run rate of growth, at least where this chart is concerned.

During to the medium-term growth stage, is the bigger threat to American growth rates a market revolt against American debt levels? Or is it structural unemployment stemming from the slow, jobless recovery? Or is the cyclical shortfall in public investment? Or something else entirely? Of course, there's no real reason one has to choose a problem to address at the expense of others. More aggressive monetary expansion could make the finding of a solution to all these problems easier, but the Fed is unwilling to oblige me on this score. It may well be concerned that lack of fiscal discipline will lead to increasing inflation expectations, making its job harder (but then fiscal problems are trace able to growth). If that is the worry, however, one has to ask why the Congress has been unable to strike a deal for $20 billion in stimulus this year for $80 billion in fiscal tightening in a year or two (fill in whatever amounts you wish). But the outlook for the American economy vis-a-vis any number of potential crises will hinge on growth, and growth will hinge on the ability of private business to exploit promising opportunities as they arise. And the question is: what's likely to hurt that ability most? High interest rates? Lack of consumer demand? A shortage of adequately prepared workers? Right now firms appear to be most worried about demand shortfalls. So how much can you boost demand without making the primary fear high interest rates? A lot, if the expansion is on the monetary side.

● How to supply consumer choice theory to predict Consumer Behavior Marketing at Apple Computer

During US economy growth, Apply computer applies consumer choice theory to solve its computer buyers' choice problems among different kinds of brand computer competitors. Have you ever wondered why Apple is so successful? They were not the first company to invent the personal computer, portable music device, the tablet, the smartphone, software to download music, or the set-top box to name a few. Apple has amassed a brand loyal following like no other brand backed by significant sales, market share, and profitability. So, how does Apple do it? What's the secret behind their success?

Marketing using consumer behavior insight is how Apple succeeds. Even though Steve Jobs and Apple, did not use consumer research in the initial development of most products, consumer behavior plays a huge role in their marketing and ultimately the success of the company. Once a consumer purchases a product or downloads iTunes Apple has access to data the company leverages. Apple uses this information to gain significant insight into the consumer and what drives purchase behavior.

Consumer behavior marketing is an essential ingredient in the current business climate. The companies that apply this type of marketing well have a distinct competitive advantage that distances them from their rivals. Consumer behavior research is the primary driver at the core of any good strategy. Research provides actionable insight and ensures business success. If you answer no to the following questions, this post is for you?

•Are you applying consumer behavior marketing currently?

•Have you conducted consumer behavior research within the last two years?

•Do you have consumer behavior marketing in your marketing plan with well-defined marketing strategies and tactics?

•Are you achieving the maximum results for your organization?

Every business has a target audience and consumer behavior marketing provides the fundamental methods for understanding your target. Consumer behavior research provides the underlying element that drives quality strategies and ensures business results.

"Marketing is understanding your buyers really, really well. Then creating valuable products, services, and information especially for them to help solve their problems."

The organizations that have an intimate understanding of their target audience possess a competitive advantage over those that do not. Establishing a one-to-one relationship and thorough knowledge of your target audience is a core responsibility for business in the 21st century and beyond. Regardless if you are B2B, B2C, B2G or a hybrid organization you have a target audience. The information in this post can be applied to any business type. This post focuses on Apple (B2C) employing consumer behavior marketing as a critical ingredient for their success.

Hence, Apply computer shops have several computer teachers to teach any visitors how to use its laptops, hen they enquire its any computer salespeople. Due to its salespeople had been trained to learn how to use the different kinds of laptops. So, anyone enquires them, they can answer their enquires concern any computer questions immediately. Then, they will feel Apple laptops are the first choice to compare other kinds of laptops brands. It is one salespeople answering strategies to persuade any Apple computer visitors to feel its any laptops are the first or preference choice to compare its competitors in this computer market, so customer choice economic theory is the most suitable strategy to solve Apple computer's customer individual purchase decision problem.

Microeconomics Models and Theories solve customer problems

Microeconomics is concerned with the economic decisions and actions of individuals and firms. Within the broad church of microeconomics, there are different theories that certain assumptions and expectations of economic behaviour. The most important theory is neo-classical theory, which places emphasis on free-markets and the assumption individuals are rational and seek to maximise utility. However, there are many critiques of the neo-classical model, arguing economics is more complex with issues of market failure and irrational behaviour.

Pre-classical microeconomic theory

Before, Adam Smith, economics was more disparate with no commanding overall theory. Philosophers like Aristotle and Plato made references to issues in economics such as division of labour. The dominant ideas, pre-classical economics, were based on theories of mercantilism – the idea a nation should try to accumulate gold.

Classical microeconomic theory

Classical microeconomic theory was developed by Adam Smith (Wealth of Nations, 1776) and later economists, such as David Ricardo The essential aspect of classical microeconomic theory include:

Adam Smith mentioned the 'invisible hand of the market.' He noted how when people act out of self-interest, markets tend to provide goods and services which are demanded by the population. It needed no central price setting, but market forces responded to changes in demand and supply, e.g. a shortage pushes up the price and causes demand to fall.

Smith also investigated topics such as the division of labour, specialisation and economies of scale. The early classical economists emphasised the importance of costs to firms and consumers.

Utility maximisation

An important development of classical economics towards the end of the nineteenth century is the concept of utility maximisation. The concept of utility was developed by philosophers/economists – Jeremy Bentham and John Stuart Mill. In microeconomic theory, it was believed a consumer will buy goods depending on the marginal utility (satisfaction) they get from the good. This theory assumes consumers are rational and seeking to maximise the satisfaction they get.

Neo-classical theory

Neo-classical theory is a modern re-interpretation of classical economics of the nineteenth century. Neo-classical theory places importance on markets, but developed new ideas, especially regarding utility and rational choice theory. Elements of neo-classical theory.

1. Market distribution of goods and services.

2.R ational choice theory. This is the idea individuals hold rational preferences and make rational choices; seeking to maximise their outcomes – be it profit, wages, consumption or investment.

3. People act independently and make use of available information.

4. Marginalism. In neo-classical economics, more emphasis was placed on concepts of marginal utility and marginal cost. We make choices depending on satisfaction we get from one extra unit of a good.

Economists such as Carl Menger, William Stanley Jevons and Marie-Esprit-Léon Walras. and Alfred Marshall developed ideas such as diminishing marginal utility. Many of these neo-classical economic theories were brought together in Alfred Marshall's very influential textbook, Principles of Economics. (1890)

•Note there is some blurring between classical economics and neo-classical economics.

•Neo-classical economics has also come to mean 'orthodox economic theory. To a large extent, it has incorporated new developments in microeconomics, such as theories of market failure, market structure and econometrics.

Theories of Market failure

Neo-classical economics has become associated with a belief in the efficiency of markets. However, microeconomic theory has also incorporated the criticisms and limitations of free-markets.

•Monopoly. Adam Smith was well aware of the problem of monopolies and how firms could use their market power to set excessive prices.

•Imperfect competition. In the 1930s, Joan Robinson developed a model of imperfect competiton, an awareness many markets were somewhere between monopoly and perfect competition often assumed in neo-classical economics.

•Externalities. Developed by Arthur C.Pigou in The Economics of Welfare (1920) this is the awareness production and consumption decisions can have harmful (or positive) effects on third parties. Therefore, a free market can lead to overconsumption of demerit goods and negative externalities.

•Game theory. An awareness, decisions are not linear or simple, but the interdependence of agents influences what we decide to do.

Behavioural economics

The most important trend in recent decades in economics is the greater emphasis placed on aspects of behavioural economics, which uses many insights from related fields such as psychology.

•Disputes rational choice theory. The essential element of behavioural economics is that it argues individual agents are often not rational and often do not seek to maximise utility.

•Behavioural economics examines how agents can be influenced by biases, and make decisions not predicted by neo-classical economic theory. Behavioural economics can explain the irrational exuberance of booms and busts.

Econometrics

In the post-war period, economics became increasingly mathematical with economists attempting to use mathematics to explain models and theories. Econometrics looks at economic data and seeks to extract simple relationships. The basic tool is the linear regression models and can be used to try and predict consumer spending and demand for labour.

Heterodox models of microeconomics

Heterodox models differ substantially from microeconomic foundations of neo-classical economics. Schools of thought include

Marxist economic theory

Karl Marx developed an alternative perspective on economics. He focused on the surplus value created under the capitalist economic system. To Marx, the invisible hand of the market would be better described as the invisible hand of capitalist exploitation of workers. Marx claimed workers did receive their full labour value but were compensated for their necessary labour only – enabling capitalists to profit from the surplus.

Institutional economics. The role of society and institutions in shaping economic behaviour. For example, Thomas Veblen looked at theories of 'conspicuous consumption' and noted how the desire for social status could drive much economic theory. Institutional economics could be seen as a forerunner for later behavioural economics.

Environmental economics Argues traditional economics wrongly places value on increasing output. The most important thing is creating a sustainable environment which maximises living standards. So, manufacturers need to consider how to manufacture their products , but pollution can not be raised as the same time, because human will face to raise cost of living and living experiences to be poor , even food shortage, water pollution , air pollution , death rate raises when technological productivities brings pollution to our natural environment. Hence, environmental economoic theory is the most suitable to solve manufacturers' pollution problem.

Buddhist economics/non-profit goals. Like environmental economics, this questions the assumption higher incomes and higher output are desirable. The theory of hedonistic relativism suggests higher incomes do nothing to increase happiness levels, and traditional economics can encourage society to pursue materialistic goals which actually create more problems of stress, conflict and environmental degradation.

Some of the basic models you might find in A-Level economics :
•Price Discrimination
•Perfect competition
•Price Mechanism
•Monopoly
•Oligopoly and kinked demand curve
•Game Theory Pricing strategies
•Market failure
•Behavioural economics

ON conclusion, any macro economy theories can be applied to find the most reasonable methods to solve any customer problems in societies by economists as above. So, I believe that any economic and customer and social problems can be solved by economic theories in our society.

Demand and supply theory solves social problems

Over the past 20 years, many researchers believe to apply behavioral economic macroeconomic models which can predict market behavioral change. The reasons are based on assumptions of optimizing behavior in many cases have difficulty accounting for key real-world observations. Hence, researchers have used behavioral economics assumptions with the aim of making their model predicting better fit the data. The reason for behavioral economics results into macroeconomics will be more accurate to predict market behavioral change in macro-economy view point, such as economic fluctuation prediction, the consumption, formation of expectations and determination of wages and employment how to aggregation supply and the possibility of consumer individual demand product or service number prediction more accurately.

● How to apply behavioral economy (demand and supply) theory to predict marketing behavioral changes more accurate?

Anyway, economists aim to develop models of human behavior and interactions in market in order to build useful models. Economists make simplifying assumptions to analyze why the market will be changed by consumer individual consumption behavior changing.

Why do I assume consumers are as economic man ? In behavioral economy view point, how the perception of the economic man's behavior (including consumer choices) of economic models with the development of economics as a science. Economists explain the concept of economics as a science. It is the concept of consumer as an economic man, the essence and complexity of consumer behavior.

The consumer and consumer purchasing behavior are an important area of interest of many scientific disciplines. The process of economic decision making as well as consumption choices are connected with wider human activities. The terms of both consumer individual attitudes and group social behavior will influence group social behavior will influence consumer individual final consumption decision in every consumption choice process. Thus, behavioral economy method can predict consumer behavioral changing, it can apply these sciences to research, includes sociology, psychology, anthropology, operational research, decision theory etc. different literature research aspects. I assume that businessmen can apply behavioral economy method to predict market changing behaviors successfully if they own behavioral economy knowledge.

In this part, I shall concentrate on explain how the perception of the economic man's behavior (including consumer choice) is applied to predict market behaviors. After explaining the concept of consumer as an economic man, the nature and complexity of consumer behavior are discussed to below different industries' marketing behavioral changing every case studies in US or UK countries.

Why is consumer as an economic man? IN behavioral economy view point, the concept of answer is one of the fundamental concepts in economics because the consumer is the case market participant along with the producer. In general, lecturers define the consumer in various ways, but in behavioral economy view point, consumers mean economy man. Because who will compare cost and benefit to any product or service to decide to choose to buy the product or consume the service. Consumers are as "economic man", who will make own subjective preferences (tastes), habits and traditions and existing objective constraints (i.e. disposal income) market prices of products and services in order to satisfy whose needs to a maximum degree and in the most rational way.

Thus, economic man means consumers need to make psychological mind to decide whether who either prefer to buy this product or another product or prefer to consume this service or another service more suitable. Thus, any markets or industries need have themselves benefits and consumers must need to evaluate whether the product or service has more benefits to compare other products or services in the consumption market to satisfy whose needs. It means that if the product or service has more benefits to compare other similar products or services. Then the product or service will persuade many consumers to choose to but the product or consume the service.

Consequently, in first part, I shall indicate how to apply behavioral economy theory : economic man psychological method, benefits and costs benefits method, how to predict these US and UK enterprises marketing behavioral changing more accurate.

In the second part, I shall apply micro employee behavioral economy concept to explain how to solve these US and UK inter-organizational management challenge.

I believe that behavioral economy method can be applied to research organizational employee behaviors change, e.g. how any why the employee chooses to do this action in whose organization. Moreover, behavioral economy method can be applied to consumption market to predict how any why the consumer choose to buy the product or consume the service. So, any consumers and employees personal psychology and external environment economic factor will influence how to choose to do decision in any organizations or consumption environment.

Bibliography

Bandiera, O., I. Barankay, and I. Rasul (2005). Social preferences and the response to incentives: Evidence from personal data. The quarterly journal of economics 120 (3), 917-969.

Exadaktylos, F., A.M. Espin and P. Branas-Garza (2013). Experimental subjects are not different. Scientific reports 3, 1213.

Lazear, E.P. (1979). Why is there mandatory retirement? Journal of political economy 87(6), 1261-1284.

● Behavioral economic method (demand and supply theory) predicts stable basic income consumer individual spending behavior

Can apply behavioral economic method to predict that the consequences of a stable basic income consumer's consumption behavior? It may be significantly different than the ones are predicted by the standard economic model if more realistic assumptions of human consumption behavioral prediction success.

Behavioral economic method assumes that consumer will compare whether whose benefits are more than costs after they buy the product or consume the service. I assume the consumer is only the who have stable basic income source consumer target. This stable basic income target consumers who will evaluate or feel they will earn more benefits than costs to every product in their consumption process, after they will make final decision to choose to buy the product to use or consume the service. Otherwise, if they feel they won't earn more benefits after they buy the product or consume the service in the consumption process. Then, they won't choose to buy the product to use or consume the service. In behavioral economic view point, it indicates their consumption behaviors are depend on comparing the product or the service whether it can satisfy their desire benefits and their desire benefits to the product or service must be more than their consumption cost.

There are four points to apply behavioral economic method to predict each stable basic income individual income spending. They include: motivation, conspicuous consumption, social preferences and crowding theory.

Each stable basic income consumer individual spending amount will be different and it is represent that every high stable basic income consumer must decide to consume any high cost services or buy high cost products to use. Although some economic teachers assume general high income people will accept to spend more expenditures for enjoyment or buy high cost of products to satisfy basic high level necessary expenditures. But, applying behavioral economic analysis, it is not absolute true, some low income people also accept to spend more to buy high cost of products or increasing spending expenditures for enjoyment for their basic necessary expenditures.

The field of behavioral economic can be fined as a combination of economics and psychology that tries to capture human behavior in a more realistic. Understanding each consumer individual consumption behavior, we need to know how who does each decision to influence each consumption choice. Consequently, analysis reaches the conclusion. Every high or low level stable basic income consumer individual behavioral consumption that the microeconomic consequences of a stable basic income of individual consumer target consumption group could be efficiency enhancing, but at the same time incentives about positional concerns could lead to wasteful and inefficient spending to the stable low basic income consumer target group.

● How to apply demand and supply theory to contribute to the stable basic income target consumer group's consumption prediction?

What is basic income mean? A basic income is an income paid by a political community to all its members on an individual basis, without means test or work requirement. How to apply behavioral economic method to contribute to the basic income consumption prediction?

I assume high income tax is charged to one high income tax payee , it will influence the high income tax payee individual consumption desires to be fallen, also extrinsic incentives will effort and intrinsic motivation and how the labor market change these variables under and big changes predicting, how income security changes social consumption preferences, e.g. how a big change affects the overall level of status -seeking behavior and this effect with income inequality to influence consumer individual consumption attitude or habit.

How can behavioral economic methods predict consumer's consumption decision, in special the stable basic income consumer target group? In any consumption decisions are involving risk and uncertainty, the standard economic model usually assumes that decisions are based on final condition, regardless of the changes are caused by the results of a consumer's decision.

An alterative mode of how consumers make decision and judgement under risk and uncertainty. This situation is often occurred in consumption market.

In behavioral economic view point, it explains how consumer's consumption, however, which excludes the stable basic income earn factor can influence the stable basic income earn target consumer group decides to make final consumption decision to compare to the non-stable basic income earn target consumer group. The reasons include as below:

(1) Consumers evaluate decisions over gains and losses with respect to some natural reference point, when they feel need to consume, which is assumed to be judgement about a sequence of outcomes are based on changes in wealth, rather than whether how much absolute basic income earn to influence whose consumption desires.

(2) Thus, behavioral economic theory assumes the consumer is the low level of income group in society, but when who feels that he is still gains more than losses when who decides to buy the expensive product or consumes the expensive service. Then, the low level of income consumer who will accept to buy the expensive product or consume the service easily. Due to whose gains feeling is more than losses feeling, when who buys the product or consumes the service.

(3) Behavioral economic theory also assumes the taxpayer will pay high income tax in this year. The, even the high income taxpayer can earn high basic income, but due to whom needs to pay high income tax in this year. Then, he/she will reduce much spending, even he/she reduces spending on cheap products or cheap service consumption for enjoyment. This is the taxpayer's economic decision to influence whose consumption behavior, due to the high income tax expenditure factor influences whose consumption behavior to change to be reduced spending expenditures in this year.

How to apply behavioral economic method to predict labor market changing behavior?

Instead of applying behavioral economic method to predict every consumer individual consumption effort. Behavioral economic method can be also be applied to predict every country's labor market changing behavior. Particularly, how salary clerical workers or low wage labor workers should move from one type of job to another based on these factors. They include as below:

Their intrinsic motivation and how their levels of effort would change after this movement, investigates the effects of income security on social preferences in labor market changing behavior, and how cooperation in social contribution is affected when income security is guaranteed, how to predict the role of positional externalities on conspicuous consumption and how would change the incentive to influence consumption. So, it seems that general labor market job changing behaviors will not influenced by external economic environment better or worse changing factor, or salary changing factor etc. different environmental condition changing factors influence to employees' job changing. Generally, employee's job changing behavior is more influenced to persuade who changes job by himself/herself intrinsic motivation negative emotion influence mainly.

How to apply motivation crowding theory to predict labor productivity? One of the main challenges of economic theory is to find what are the optimal incentives that increase productivity of labors. The standing point is usually extrinsic incentive be it is form of monetary compensations for high effort or fine for low effort.

It is a kind method of reward or punishment to increase or decrease number of productivity to every labor. But it can only raise short term number of productivity in possible and it can not guarantee high quality of productivity. So if one employer wants a labor to do more of an activity or with a higher quality, consider paying the labor for working hard on punishing whom if for providing a low level effort.

This idea is that people do not like to work, and therefore they used some sort of compensation for doing a specific activity, and that the more they are paid the harder, they will work. So, payment better compensation is only beneficial to encourage labors to do one specific task or activity in short term. This method can not be suitable to rise long term beneficial productivity and high level quality of production or excellent performance in long term and it can only keep in short term raising productivity and high level quality of production or excellent performance benefits.

Consider paying the labor for working hard on punishing whom if for providing a low level effort. This idea is that people do not like to work, and therefore they used some sort of compensation for doing a specific activity, and that the more they are paid the harder they will work. So, payment better compensation is only beneficial to encourage labors to do one specific task or activity in short term. This method can not be suitable to raise long them beneficial productivity and high quality of products.

However, economists would argue that, is a labor has high intrinsic motivative to perform a task, who will provide a high level of effort without compensation by himself/herself but an even higher level of effort of whom is compensated. If a labor does not have any intrinsic motivation to perform a task or an activity, who will provide no effort or a low effort of whom. There is no compensation, but who will increase this level of effort of an extrinsic incentive is implemented.

Hence, in behavioral economic view point, the labor individual high level effort is a main psychological factor to influence whose productivity to be raised or the qualities of products to be raised, when the products are manufactured by the high level effort labor. It means that high compensation is not the good method to encourage labor productivity or raise quality. Otherwise, how to influence the one low level of effort of labor to change to be one high level of effort labor. It is the best psychological method to influence the labor to raise productivity and quality and service performance to any products or services in manufacturing process or service process for any organizations in long term beneficial possible.

● How can apply demand and supply theory raises basic stable income consumer consumption desire

Economists aim to develop models of human behavior and interactions in consumption markets. But consumers behave in complex ways, such as how to predict consumers to make rational decisions in consumption processes. Moreover, self-consumption control and motivation can vary significantly across different individual consumer.

In order to build useful consumption prediction models, economists make simplifying assumptions, aims to predict how to raise stable basic income consumer target group consumption more success. However, behavioral economy method is one kind of accurate consumption prediction method. It can be applied to predict economic decision-making to every consumer consumption choice more accurate raising whose consumption desire?

I shall indicate how to apply different behavioral economy methods (demand and supply theory) to raise stable basic stable income target consumer group consumption desire in these different consumption situation (consumption environment) aspects as below:

1. Stable basic stable income consumer group consumption great or small amount desire

The consumption of products and services is a fundamental part of consumer's welfare. Basically, every one who has stable basic stable income, who will like to consume any products and services. Even, consumption great or small amount desire won't be depended on whether the person whose income is more or less. It means low income level of people will still like to consume great amount to buy expensive products or consume expensive services, because consumption is human's part of life and basic needs.

This stable basic income people will like to consume, because they have stable income source when they do not worry about unemployment occurrence to cause them have no enough money to support their life. Otherwise, non-stable basic stable income people won't like to consume because they feel they have no stable basic income source to support their life and they will worry about unemployment occurrence any time. Hence, stable basic income people will have more consumption desire to compare non-stable basic stable income people in any countries usually. Behavioral economic method indicates they feel their economic benefits will be loss if they planned to buy any products or consume any services easily. So, they prefer to save money in bank more than consumption.

1. Demand systems and micro-economic factor influence basic income people consumption attitude

Why stable basic income people will like to consume? Because who have more demand, a demand system shows the level of consumer demand for different products and services: e.g. one basic stable income person may refer to the demand for clothes, another the demand for food etc.

How the demand for that particular product varies with the prices and demographic factor will influence who to accept consumption. Such as stable basic income people who will not consider to decide to buy the cloth to wear or the food to eat if who feel the cloth or food price is even more expensive to compare other kind of cloth or food.

Otherwise, non-stable basic income people who will consider to decide to buy the cloth to wear or the food to eat if they feel that they still have enough cloths to wear or enough food to eat at homes , even these food or cloth price are less expensive to compare others. Because they feel they lack stable income effort to support them to consume. Hence, basic stable income factor can influence the consumer's consumption decision.

2. Life-cycle advertisement method can influence consumer individual consumption behaviors to be increased

Consumer behavior makes strong assumptions about the informational and computational bases of consumer behavior. Generally, consumer behavior is reasonably characterized as the maximization of expected lifetime utility subject to budget constraint and conditional on the available information.

Generally, consumers prefer to buy any discounted products or it is reasonable that consumers accept to buy many attractions to persuade them to buy any kinds of bargain discount products. Hence, low bargain discount product is one good behavioral economic principle to encourage or persuade or attract any consumers to increase consumption.

What is behavioral life-cycle model? This model explains consumer behavior can be persuaded to buy any discounted products by advertisement, e.g. television, radio, newspapers, magazine etc. promotion channels. Because frequent advertisement promotion method can let any consumers often remember the product's brand, discounted price, style, color and image from advertisement content.

So, advertisement can be one part of consumer behavioral life-cycle. For example, when the television audiences often watch TV. Hence, when the brand of product advertisement often makes fun image and discounted message to let TV audiences to remember this brand of product, when they are watching TV. Then, it has possible to persuade any potential consumers to choose to buy this brand of any products or consume this brand of any services, due to its advertisement of discounted sale message is very attractive to every one to let this advertisement audience's attention to remember this brand of products or services are selling or serving in market at this moment. So, it is advertisement image behavior influences audiences to buy the brand's any products attractively and persuasively.

3. Raising electricity consumption from electricity user individual habit

For electricity use market case example, how to analyze people's behavior in consuming electricity using a behavioral economic framework ? Electricity consumption is modeled by the means of consumer's individual useful habit, electricity price, consumer satisfaction level, willingness to invest in new technologies, social interactions, and marketing strategies by the power utility. Because electricity is necessary to every home or electric vehicle users needs or businessmen office etc. different needs every day.

Power companies supply electricity to a region's homes and industries. However, electricity needs modernization of power system companies expect to increase price. Due to competitive factor, such as other fuel resource choices, outdated kind of energy electricity supply, and renewable fuel energy source competition.

Hence, applying behavioral economic concept, I assume electricity consumers will compare to electricity and other kinds of energy choices to weigh up the costs and benefits of all alternatives, aiming to maximize their benefits, before making a decision to choose to use electricity for their house electricity demand or electric vehicle or shop or factory manufacturing etc. function of different aspects of electricity users.

For example, electricity business clients, they aim to reduce cost, such as energy expenditure, when they use any energy to manufacture their products in factories. If they feel electricity is expensive price to compare other kinds of energy power supply. When, they feel that they can not earn much beneficial advantages to use electricity to produce their products. Otherwise, if they feel other any kinds of energy supply can replace electricity to give more benefits to compare electricity energy. Then, many business electricity users will change to use other kinds of energies to consume to replace electricity power.

However, electricity can have competitive ability in electric vehicles market, if many drivers feel environment protection is more important to compare vehicles will be popular to be driven, due to many drivers don't want air pollution. They will like gas vehicles. Hence, the main attribute from the consumer side is one their habit electricity consumption behaviors, satisfaction level, energy efficient interaction with the power utility.

Consequently how to predict electricity consumer's demand. The important factor is how to let electricity users to feel power companies are changing a reasonable level to compare other similar energy supply products. When electricity users feel electricity which can bring more benefits to compare other kinds of energy products. Then, in energy supply market, if the demanding number of electricity consumers can increase more than other kinds of energy demanding number. Then, it is right time to raise electricity price to charge electricity consumers. Hence, how to persuade electricity consumers to feel that they can have more benefits to compare other kinds of energy products. It is the main successful factor to electricity power supply companies.

● Consumer confidence is as a predictor of consumption spending

Behavioral economists believe it has link between confidence and economic decisions to cause consumers to choose spending, if the consumer has confidence to believe the product is worth to use, then who will accept to buy the product to use.

Concentrated on the conceptualization of confidence and its role in mode in theories of consumption. It also concerns on whether the confidence indicators contain any information beyond economic fundamentals. The concern is whether confidence can be explained by current and past value of variables, such as income, unemployment, inflation or consumption or in other way.

Whether confidence measures have any statistical significance in predicting economic outcomes once information from the above variables is used. Economic variable factor will also influence consumer confidence to decide consumption spending, e.g. real consumption expenditures (income, wealth or interest rate).

Finally, it will identify under which circumstances confidence indicates can be a good predictor of household consumption. Hence, survey is one good measurement method to predict whether how much every household has confidence to spend to consume the brand of products to use. Why is survey a good confidence consumption measurement prediction to every household in every country?

The reasons include survey can gather every household consumption habit history data to evaluate whether every survey person has how much confidence to consume the brand of products. Which in most cases correspond to periods where there are large changes in household survey indicators, liking during financial crises or geopolitical tensions to measure or predict whether the country's future good or bad economic condition factor will influence every household consumption desire in the year.

This modelling approach assumes that there is a certain (unknown) in confidence index changes beyond which confidence starts impacting consumption behaviors. So, sample household surveys can show the contribution of confidence in explaining consumption expenditures increases when household survey indicators feature large changes. So that confidence indicators can have some increasing predictive power during the survey investigation period in the year.

Other view point, surveys have been concerned on whether the confidence indicators contain any information beyond economic fundaments. The concern is whether confidence can be explained by current and past values of variables, such as income, unemployment, inflation or consumption or the other way. Whether confidence measures have any statistical significance in predicting economic outcomes once information from different external variable factors to influence the survey household group.

What is confidence in consumption survey ?

Confidence in consumption. For example, to measure whether how much degree of strong inflation in the economy, such as recessions and recoveries will influence the country's household confident consumption in the year. The surveys consumers' questions usually concern on major expenditures and changes in the respondent's financial situation, focus on job availability and current business conditions etc. questions. It is then possible that about consumer confidence depending on the relative performance of the variables that may be more relevant balances, with respect to the factors that determine unemployment and other labor market related issues. It aims to investigate whether those any one of variable factors will influence consumers general loss confident consumption desire in this year.

What is a confidence indicator ?

A confidence indicator is considered as an explanatory variable for consumption together with standard variables used on predicting consumption expenditure. However, the natural real personal consumption expenditure is unexpected and unpredicted easily.

In conclusion, consumption expenditure depends the consumer individual confidence. If the consumer has much confidence to feel this year economic change will be better and he/she is easily to find job, then he/she will accept consumption easily in this year. It seems financial wealth and unemployment etc. economic factors will influence every household consumption desire. So, survey is one kind of good psychological consumption prediction method to predict consumption spending for any country in the year. I recommend manufacturers may choose to apply survey method to attempt to enquire sample survey people to gather data to predict whether what degree of consumption desire to them and find solution methods to solve low degree of consumption desire challenge.

How to apply behavioral economy methods to influence employee individual psychology to achieve raise productivity of long term incentive intention?

Increasing salary is short term incentive productivity method. Behavioral economy assumes labors will choose to do beneficial behaviors to themselves when they feel their work behaviors can earn more benefits to themselves more than their employers in the organizations. Otherwise, if they feel their work behaviors can earn more benefits to their employers more than themselves. Then, they won't choose to do their work behaviors, e.g. raising productivities or work hard. Due to they feel work hard or raise productivities behaviors that only give more benefits to their employers more themselves.

Whether does cheap product price incentive consumption desire to influence effective consumption behavior? Whether is monetary increasing salary payment incentive labors might be willing to work on task? I feel raising labors productivities is similar to raise incentive consumption, which both have similar point, such as increasing salary payment or cheap product price is the main factor to influence incentive consumption or raising productivities. Hence, it seems monetary factor is not the main effort to encourage labors to work hard.

In labor's behavioral economic view point, for example, if an employer pays an employee more doing a task, who might be less willing to work on it, who might be less productive given whose efforts and who may enjoy the task less. If you want your employees to save more for retirement. You may want to give them fewer investment options. If you want them to engage more in a task, you might want offer them an additional alternative, instead of increasing salary to that task. Thus, increasing salary is not only method to encourage productivities of incentives.

How to improve the design of incentive structures to encourage productivities in any organizations?

Any monetary incentive can only encourage productivities in short term. It can not only encourage productivities in long term in any organizations. It is similar to cheap or discount product price can only attractive consumers to buy the product in short term, it can not attract consumers to choose to buy the product in long term, it prefers to have more options to encourage labors to incentive productivities, e.g. investing good beneficial retirement plans. Suggesting that employees do not have free disposal of their investment options. These standard incentives seem irrelevant raising salary monetary factor, they can be quite effective in inducing labors to take particular actions to incentive productivities in long term. Due to when they can hard work, then they have more beneficial retirement plans or investing plans for their retirement. It means when they can achieve the most effective or efficient productivities to the employer for long term. It will give better retirement benefits and investment benefits to the better or even the best performance of employees. Otherwise, the worst performance employees won't earn good retirement benefits and investment benefits, when their employers feel their perform very poor in the organizations in long term.

Hence, increasing salary level method is not one successful long term incentive method to persuade every employee to raise productivities or encourage excellent performance optional method. Increasing salary level is only similar to reduce product price and it is only short term encouragement to consumption or productivities method.

In conclusion, extrinsic monetary factor can not incentive labor's raising productivities more than every employee themselves intrinsic motivation to raise productivities as excellent performance in any organizations. Thus, organizations need to let employees to feel that they can give long term economic benefits to encourage their intrinsic motivation effort to be raised their productivities or performance more effective or efficient in order to achieve long term both win-win economic benefits to employees and employers both.

Building employees and managers kindly co-operational relationship method

If you are an economist, your employer has no without any financial incentive to encourage your economic research tasks in your organization. It is equally difficult to certify that such activity will contribute to your growth of human capital and increased productivity in research or teaching. The standard model, which explains employee's effort only through the way (determined by productivity), is therefore incomplete. In particular, it doesn't consider that incentives to work do not have to be monetary in other words, that there are other things besides the disutility of labor (Kamenica, 2012) and section 1.3 have.

Why will short term wage increasing method only influence short term labor supply to raise productivities? The effect of reference raising wage can be most easily identified on short term labor supply to raise productivities. For US, New York city taxi drivers case, they have to decide every day for low long they are going to offer their services, given the day-to-day variable ability of demand they face (peaking during bad weather and/or when big conferences and public events are taking place in the city).

In the standard model, houses worked should grow with any growth in demand for New York taxi drivers' services. (one day's earning will have only a negligible income effect in the longer run). And yet actual cabbies work less on a demand heavy day. One of possible explanations suggests that New York city taxi drivers expect a certain income, they have set themselves a specific target income, who expect to achieve every day. During low demand for their taxi services, then they work longer hours to reach the target, when during peak demand, their referential income is achieved quickly and they only work short hours. Elasticity of hours worked with respect to their earnings is therefore negative (Lamerer, Babcock, Loewenstein, & Thaler, 1997).

However, taxi driver is either one self employment business or one taxi company employment driving service occupation. It is similar to other kinds of service jobs in societies. Servicing employees, such as waiters, salespeople, securities, customer services, bus drivers etc. different kinds of service occupations. They are not similar to manufacturing occupation to be applied how many amount of piece of products production to evaluate their productivities efforts. Thus these any one of service job nature is depended on their service performance to clients to feel their service performances are excellent to compare general service performance effort of service employees.

Considerably, respectively, I assume that if these service employees' managers can build kindly working environment, e.g. manager individual attitude and behavior can let their employees to feel happy to work together in their teams. Then, the managers' kindly as enthusiastic behaviors or attitudes will let every employee more positive encouragement of service attitude to serve their clients in their teams. Then, the client complaining number will be possible reduced, even none of any complains. Hence, building kindly relationship between managers and employees will raise excellent service performance to any organization service nature employees.

Can bonus method encourage service performance to be raised ?

In service job nature of bonus method can also raise employees' overall productivities or service performance. For example, when employees got a provisional bonus before the start of the workweek, but were warned that they would lose it on payday, unless they achieve the productivities or excellent service performance norm, they worked more productivities or let many clients to satisfy their service performance. Hence, managers can achieve bonus plan to compensate any excellent productivity or excellent services to them. Then, they can let clients to feel their service performance more satisfactory than employees of a control group who were merely given the standard promise to receive a bonus upon achieving the norm.

The effort was relatively small, however, productivity grew 1%. Interestingly, the effect of a loss was stronger when how teams were rewarded this way, social pressure came to bear on the less productivity team members. When the team members won't earn any bonus. So, long-term productivity gains were achieved through bonuses paid by excellent performance compensation method to compare to low service performance employees receiving no bonuses at all.

Economic views of human motivation nature

There are only two main types of economic actors and by making simplifying assumptions about how these types of actors behave and interact. The two basic sets of actors in this model are firms, which are assumed in this model are firms, which are assumed to maximize their profits from producing and selling products and services, households, which are assumed to maximize their utility (or satisfaction) from consuming products and services.

It seems any employees will choose to do behaviors to achieve to earn much benefits from their organizations. The models of economic behaviors that consider considerate employees' choice of goals, the actions they take to achieve these goals and the limitations and influences that affect their choices and actions.

For university students choose which universities to study case, suppose that any college enrollment students are deciding which courses to study. Thus, it implies that if the university can provide many different kinds of suitable or right courses to any college enrollment students to choose to study. It means that if the university can provide many different kinds of courses to enrollment students to choose to study. Then, it will have much chance to attract enrollment students to choose this university to study. It's competition can be raised by many courses choice factor. but, in fact, it is not absolute right, although the university can provide many courses to provide to enrollment students to choose to study. But, it is not guarantee to represent it must attract many students to enroll this university to study.

For example, suppose that college enrollment students are deciding which courses to choose to study. Although, it has right course to prepare to these enrollment students to choose to study. But, they see a summary of evaluations from hundreds of other students indicating that a certain course is very good in this university. Then, suppose that they match a video interview of just one student to give a negative review of this university of the course. Even when students were told in advance that such a negative review was worse to this university of the course. They tended to be more influenced by the negative review than the summary of hundreds of evaluations, even although such behavior seems irrational. Hence, although many right courses choice has much chance to attract students to enroll this university to study. But, if its bad educational quality from this course from negative review factor, which will influence the enrollment students number to be reduced.

It implies that students will compare this university's the course educational quality whether is better or worse to compare other universities' similar course educational quality, even this university's this course fee whether is reasonable in educational market. This is cost and beneficial comparison behavioral economy principle to all enrollment students before they decide to choose which universities.

Hence, this case implies that universities how to train teachers' teaching skills to let students to feel that they can learn new knowledge from their teaching staffs absolutely. It means how to raise education training skills to raise teachers' teaching performance. It is very important factor to influence the university's teaching development success. So, many courses choice is not important factor to attract many students to enroll the university. Otherwise, although the university can not provide many courses to let students to enroll, but it's teachers can provide excellent teaching service to teach whose students. This is important factor to attract many students to choose to enroll this university to study.

Under-level productive efficiency and low-consumption desire behavioral economic influences

In behavioral economic influence view point, I feel that under-level productive efficiency is the represent low production number to the manufacturer as well as low-consumption desire is not represent less consumers demands or customers lose confidence to the product.

On the one hand, I shall apply behavioral economic method to analyze why under productive efficiency is not represent low production number influence. Otherwise, I feel under-productive efficiency will have possible to increase production number after the manufacturer can review what factor(s) to influence under-productive efficiency.

I shall give reasons to explain as below:

As Jim, P. & Brendan. M. (2013) indicated who had ever been experiencing failure to do their businesses. Although, they had lost a million dollars, but they felt that they can be taught to learn undiscovered knowledge to know how to do their businesses successful by their wrong judgement and decision learning experience. They explained that " in ll risk taking, speculation, business ventures, entrepreneurial activities, it is the loss side on which you must focus first. This is even true for gambling, the gambler determines how much he's willing to bet, and loss, before the game is played. He doesn't wait for the game to end and then let the croupier or dealer assign his wager for him. How do you determine the downside, and how do you control or minimize it? With objective decision making and a plan that has as its starting point the stop-loss parameters"

Hence, it explains any business will have under-level productive efficiencies and low consumption desire business risk. However, to any one entrepreneur, who needs to know it is one game between the himself/herself and whose clients. They also need to know with objective decision making and a plan that has as its starting point.

Hence, I assume that if the entrepreneur has wrong decision to cause under-level productive efficiency, it is possible that, due to there is no enough employee number to manufacture the product or many employees are not skillful to manufacture all product in normal time or many employees are lazy etc. different factors to cause under-level productivities. However, when they discover their productivities are very low to compare similar competitors their employees' productivities and efficiencies. Then, they can attempt to find what factor(s) to cause low productivities and low efficiencies. it is possible that any one among of these factors case. They include many employees' lazy to influence low productivities or there is no enough employee number or many employees are not skillful to manufacture their products in production process.

Hence, wrong decision or plan is not represent failure. Otherwise, it can give chance to let the entrepreneur to learn whether what the factor(s) is (are) to cause low productivities and low efficiencies in whose product manufacturing process. As I feel that under-level productive efficiency is not represent low production number. Because I assume that if one worker lacks enough skills and manufacturing experiences to manufacture the product, but who can spend less time to manufacture the product and whose spending manufacturing time is same to the another owning enough skillful worker's time to do the product. Hence, I believe that the product quality from the low-skillful worker's manufacturing skill, it's quality will be worse to compare to the product quality from the high skillful worker's manufacturing skill. Hence, if the low skillful worker needs to spend much time to produce the product, but the product quality can be same to the high skillful worker's product quality. It means that it is sure because the low skillful worker has no excellent skill to compare to the high skillful worker to produce the product. Hence, his manufacturing spending time must be longer than the high skillful worker's time. It implies that the low skillful worker spends less time to raises high production number, but his product must be poor quality to sell. Then, his fast and efficient manufacturing speed that is not achieve economic beneficial to the organization's manufacturing process, e.g. less electricity spends to manufacture the product. Otherwise, the low skillful worker's fast and efficient manufacturing speed of behavior will raise the organization's cost in manufacturing process because consumers would not like to choose to buy any low quality product when they can choose which similar products to compare which one has the best quality and cheap price to buy.

Hence, efficient production is not the main factor to influence the business's success. Otherwise, good quality of the product factor is more important to compare it to influence the business's success.

On the other hand, I shall apply behavioral economic theory to analyze why low-consumption desire is not represent consumer demand lose to the business. As Jim. P. & Brendan. M. (2013) also identified " rather than looking for success to follow, who explained the formula for failure to avoid. As an Wang, founder of Wang laboratories said " it is my belief that there are no secret to success." The formula for failure is not lack of knowledge, brains, skills or hard work and it's not lack of luck, it's personalizing losses, especially of preceded by a string of wins or profits. It's refusing to acknowledge and accept the reality of a loss when it starts to occur because to so so would reflect negatively on you."

Thus, as whose feeling to explain why low-consumption desire is not represent less consumers demands or customers lose confidence to the product. The reasons include the causes of low-consumption desire are possible due to worse economic environment factor influences consumption desire to be reduced. It is not due to whether the product price is too high or quality is worse to compare others. Hence, as Jim & Brendan indicated the formula for business failure is not lack of knowledge, brains, skills or hard work and it's not lack of luck. It's not lack of luck. It's personalizing losses, means its reflecting to knowledge and accept the reality of a loss when it starts to occur. As it is applied to explain why low-consumption desire is not represent less consumers demands or customers lose confidence to the product. It's possible that external economic environment changing worse factor to cause the business personalizing losses, it is not reflect who lacks knowledge, skill, hard work factors to cause failure. Hence, ho to predict when and how and why economic environment changes worse will be important factor to predict when and how and why consumption behavioral changes to cause business's success.

● Demand and supply theory solves organizational problems

Any organizations can let salespeople feel happy to sell their products. Then their sale performance will also raise. The question concerns that how to make them to feel happy to help the organization to sell their products? I shall explain some methods as below:

How to manage sales for predictable revenue? In order to hold salespeople sale psychology whether they feel happy or unhappy, executives need to understand the essential activities, sales managers must focus on to be analysts for change, foster continuous improvement and create a sales culture that drives results. Sale executives need to know how to achieve top objectives of sales management is to drive sales, capture new revenue and exceed monthly sales and margin objectives, e.g. performing sale straregy development with each salesperson on Monday morning at a minimum, and in a formal one-on-one meeting during the week;using strategy tools and questioning techniques to ensure the prospects are qualified and the strategy is valid; knowing the ratio between future values and future monthly quotos to raise sale opportunities; six month on-going sale plan aims to make sure there are coordinated to achieve sale to various market segments; developing on ongoing series of networking events to build market awareness in order to ensure all salespeople attend specific events involved in networking by salespeople to, understanding the market how to influence salespeople sale method to sale number, understanding trends and seeking some channels to raise additional sales opportunities; how to create trained or warm sale environment to let sales teams feel happy to sell.

How to design and utilize efficient control sale procedures? The sale cycle procedure may include these market activities, such as advertising, sales promotion, market research, physical distribution, pricing , sale place, sale staffs seeking. SO, any organizations need have good sale planning, direction and control of the personnel, selling activities of a business with including recruiting, selecting, training, rating, supervising, paying or reward system, motivating strategy , as all these tasks apply to the personnel sales-force.

The factors may influence salespeople psychology, they may include fair income reward system, or appreciation methods and sale career development plan to every salesperson. It aims to encourage them to achieve the highest sale effort. Anymore, methods to train sale managers have the right direction to guide, lead and motivate their salespeople, e.g.

knowledge of salespeople psychology needs how to satisfy them, understanding why they choose to do or act themselves sale behaviors in order to improve their weakness to motivate salespeople to achieve company's sale target goal every month easily, e.g. raising profitability, sales volume, market share, growth and corporate image building raise clients' confidence to choose to buy this company's any products more easily.

The sales organization is required for the following purposes, they may include: enabling top-management, to devote to more time in policy making for the growth and expansion of business to divide and fix authority among the subordinates , so that they may shirk work, to avoid repetition of duties and functions, so that there may not be any confusion among them to locate responsibility of each and every employee , so that they can complete the whole work in stipulated time, if not then the particular person must be responsible, to establish the sales effort to enforce proper supervision of sales force.

What does the concept of salespeople replacement value mean? What is a sales force turnover management tool? Sales force turnover is defined as the rate at which salespeople leave an organizations, resignations, retirements or dismissals. So, if the organization can raise the sales force turnover ratio, because many salespeople can be promoted or the retirement, or the sales force turnover ratio raising reasons as well as they are not resignation or dismissal reasons. I believe that the organization ought have good sale environment and reasonable reward and welfare strategy to let its salespeople feel happy to help this company to sell its products every day.

However, sales management's actions have direct or indirect effects to impact on turnover. Direct effects may include the firm's firing or dismiss policy. The indirect effects on sale turnover may include new salesperon recruiting and selecting policies affect the quality and performance of the sale force as well as the speed at which salespeople are replaced. The same policies have an impact on the sales force turnover rate through the characteristics of the newly recurited salespersons and the promotion , training, retraining policies, support, supervision, compensation. ALl of those factors have an impact on salesperson's personal satisfaction or dissatisfaction absolutely. So, any sale organizations need to concern how and why whether any one of above these factors may influence their salespeople how to perform or act sale behaviors in order to excite their sale number more effective in long term.

How to achieve sale force management effectively? Sale management is one strategy to many organizations, because organizations expect their salespeople can only raise product sale number. So , they will consider whetther how to implement the sale management strategy to be the most suitable to themselves sale organizations in order to excite their sale teams to sell their products to achieve sale growth aim effectively. So for organization's long term sale growth development, it seems that one excellent sale management strategy can help the organization has stable sale number growth in long term possible.

However, the term " selling" includes a variety of sales situations and activities. For example, those sales positions where the sales representative is required primarily to deliver the product to the customer on a regular or periodic basis. The emphasis is this type of sales activity is very different to the sales position where the sales representative is dealing with sales of capital equipment to industrial purchasers. IN additions some sales representatives deal only in export markets whereas others sell direct to customers in their homes. So, sale organizations need to sell to local or overseas market as well as its target customer is businessmen or individual consumer or both in order to implement to choose their most suitable sale management strategy to train their salespeople more effective or achieving sale growth objective only. Because these its sale major target and where sale market place both factors will influence how it ought train its salespeople, so any organization's training method ought be influenced to change by whom is its major sale target and where is its major sale market location factors.

How to know the psychology of salesmanship? WHen the organization can predict or find reasons to explain why its salespeople feel unhappy to help
this organization to sell its products. Then, it can attempt to improve its weaknesses in order to let its salespeople to feel more sale service satisfactory feeling to continue to help this organization to sell its products. THen, it won't need not often to train or recruit new salespeople to replace its old salespeople in consequence. How to know what its salespeoples' real need in order to raise their sale service satisfactory feeling ?

Psychology means that " science of the mind" and psychology plays to important part in business and it is quite worth to bring to influence any organization salespeoples' posivitive or negative sale emotion in their every sale process between themselves and their every client in personal. For example, if the salesperson often have negative emotion or he feels unhappy in every sale process, then he will encounter or increase many times of sale failure possibilities. He will feel that he is one poor verbal advertiser or seller or promotor to help his organization to promote its products to sell again as well as he will lose confidence to sell any products next sale chance, because his failure sale experiences are accumulated to influence his sale emotion to be poor or difficult sale.

Hence, the poor performance salesperson needs have more successful sale experiences to compensate his / her prior many sale failure times feeling, if the organization hopes this poor performance salesperson can raise sale number easily. Overall, any organizations need to concern how to improve or raise the more failure times of sale experience salespeoples' sale techniques or methods or attitudes more than choose to fire or dismiss them as well as finding another new salesperson to replace him/her. Because it is possible that the salesperson 's poor sale performance that is not due to himself/herself poor sale effort and sale knowledge or lacking sale experience to the product, it may be due to the poor sale team cooperation relationship , feeling poor or not comfortable sale physcial shop environment, poor sale manager and other salespeople working relationship, the sale manager lacks leadership effort, poor family relationship etc. external factors more than himself/herself personal poor or negative emotion or poor health etc. personal factors. Hence, the organization ought enquire him/her why he/she feels unhappy to sell its products and it needs to attempt to find methods to solve his/her challenges immediately. If his/her challenges can be solved. It is possible that his/her sale efforts can be also raised for. So, if the organization can know how to utilize positive sale emotion psychological methods to predict or know why and how every salesperson perform his/her sale behavior in whose daily sale tasks, then it can concentrate on implementing effective and the most suitable sale training to raise their sale abilities more easily.

However, the sale training may include: How to build or improve long term good salesperson and his/her customer sale service relationship between every salesperson and every client in every buying and selling cycle process, how to using right communicating styleds for better understanding every client's real needs, powers and negotiating, e.g. every salesperson needs to review why there are many clients do not choose to buy any products from his sale presentation or promotion, finding every time sale failure reasons can let the salesperson makes himself/herself sale failure reasons evaluation or judgement in order to find what is the major reason influences his/her sale failure, e.g. lacking product knowledge, he/she often let many clients to feel that he lacks patience to listen the client's enquiry or feedback, his sale presentation is not attractive to let many clients like to stay longer time to listen his sale presentation in whole sale process, the salesperson himself/herself emotion is negative and he /she can let many clients feel he / she is not happy or does not enjoy to sell this product from himself/herself face impression or sale behavior impression easily, lacking enough sale techniques to persuade his/her clients why he/she ought choose to buy this product in whole sale process etc. these factors may influence the salesperson's sale failure chance to be raised. Hence sales manager ought need to spend long time to meet the poor sale performance salesperson to discuess what his/her sale challenges are the most major to influence his/her every sale successful chance in order to improve his/ her sale performance more successfully.

ON conclusion, the reasons why salespeople often encounter sale failure possibilities. The factors may include these aspects, such as they lask the desire to help customers to make satisfactory purchase decisons, they only concern how to achieve sale final objective or aim only, it will cause clients feel they do not real concern their real needs. They only concern to sell the product in success. They do not know how to describe the product whether what characteristics or features it owns accurately in order to increase sale chance to persudade them to make final decision to by the product, they do not attempt to participate the whole sale process to help them to choose the most right product in order to satisfy their any purcahse needs, they ought avoid deceptive or manipulative influence tactics, avoid the use of high pressure sales techniques etc. Thus, if any organizations can spend time to investigate what factors cause why any one of salespeople choose perform his/her sale behavior often in order to know or understand their salespeople' sale psychology absolutely. Then, I believe that their sale number will only grown more easily.

www.ingramcontent.com/pod-product-compliance
Lightning Source LLC
Chambersburg PA
CBHW061319120726
48001CB00002B/594